CITIZEN

DIPLOMACY

CITIZEN DIPLOMACY

RESPONDING TO QUESTIONS ABOUT AMERICA

DAVID M. KENNEDY
CENTER FOR
INTERNATIONAL STUDIES

BRIGHAM YOUNG UNIVERSITY
PROVO, UTAH

Library of Congress Cataloging-in-Publication Data

Citizen diplomacy: responding to questions about America

    223 p.

Updated edition of: Citizen ambassadors / by Charles T. Vetter Jr. ©1983.

    Includes bibliographical references.
    ISBN: 0-912575-15-8

    1. United States—Miscellanea. 2. United States—Relations—Foreign countries—Miscellanea. I. Vetter, Charles T.—Citizen ambassadors. II. David M. Kennedy Center for International Studies.

E156.C58   1995
973—dc20   95-38762
                                                           CIP

David M. Kennedy Center for International Studies, Brigham Young University
©1995 by Brigham Young University. All rights reserved
Printed in the United States of America
97   2

Distributed by Brigham Young University,
Kennedy Center Publications, PO Box 24538, Provo, UT 84602-4538
Phone: (800) 528-6279; Fax: (801) 378-5882; Web: www.byu.edu/culturgrams

CONTENTS

LIST of QUESTIONS

11. Why is there such prejudice and hate between whites, blacks, and other ethnic groups in America?

12. Why are Indians among some of the poorest in your country?

13. Why are Americans so "open" and extroverted—willing and anxious to talk about very personal things in public?

14. Why do Americans rely so much on psychotherapy and drugs? Why is there such a market for illegal drugs? I'm aware that my country supplies yours with drugs, but we wouldn't if the United States didn't provide such a large market.

15. Do American television shows and movies accurately portray American life? Why do you export your media? Many people in my country feel the U.S. media corrupts our youth; plus it gives Americans a bad image.

16. Why are Americans obsessed with health and fitness? Why are they so worried about their appearance?

17. Why are American sports so violent?

18. Don't you live in a very materialistic, "throw-away" society?

19. Americans seem to be better "doers" than "thinkers." On the whole, they seem more pragmatic than spiritual and philosophical. Is this an accurate assessment?

20. Why aren't more Americans interested in and informed about what happens outside your country's borders? Even your news focuses mainly on national events.

21. Why don't Americans learn our language and more about our culture while they are here? Why don't people from the United States living in our country socialize or mix with our people?

22. Whom do Americans most admire? Who are their heroes?

CHAPTER TWO:
AMERICAN GOVERNMENT

23. With such diversity in your population, how can you have only a two-party political system?

24. How do people become president in your country? Some of your past presidents appear to have had little practical political experience: Carter was a peanut farmer, Reagan was an actor, and Clinton didn't serve in the U.S. military.

25. If yours is a participatory form of government, why don't more people vote in elections? In our country it's a law to register and vote.

26. How does your government function?

27. Is the American government responsive to the needs of the people?

28. If America is one of richest nations, why can't it balance its budget?

29. How can you have good security for diplomacy and intelligence with your Freedom of Information Act and government officials and journalists who reveal government secrets?

30. Is your CIA really necessary in the post-Cold War environment?

31. Is it true that millions of your own people can't afford medical care? Why don't you have a government health-care program? You say you are against socialism, but in this case, socialized medicine would seem more humane.

32. If you have a democratic constitution, why have your people had to fight for civil and equal rights?

33. How can the American government—which protests human-rights violations in other countries—uphold capital punishment within its own borders?

34. How does your government take care of your unemployed? your poor?

35. How do you get your people to pay taxes? Why are your taxes so much lower than ours?

36. What role does religion play in American politics?

37. Is it true that your government funds abortion? How do Americans feel about that?

38. What role does the U.S. government play in organizing and financing your educational system?

60. Why does America impose economic sanctions on countries in response to noneconomic situations, such as "undemocratic practices" and "human-rights violations?" Do they really work?

61. How do you explain America's inconsistent policy on sanctions against countries with human-rights abuses, authoritarian juntas, etc.?

62. Why does the United States measure other countries by its yardstick with regards to human rights and democracy? Don't you realize strong measures are needed to provide security in some nations?

63. Many say America's position on human rights is hypocritical since you still discriminate against minorities in your country. Why does your country police some nations when it is not completely democratic? How does the United States justify passing judgment on other countries?

64. Why do you continue to pressure and isolate Cuba, even though the Soviet threat no longer exists? You even reconciled with China.

65. Will the Middle East peace process that America helped initiate work? What would the United States do to ensure peace comes to the Palestinians and Israelis? Haven't you consistently favored Israel and not adequately considered the Palestinians?

66. Why are Americans so anti-immigrant? Why do your immigration policies discriminate against immigrants from certain countries?

67. Why do you send ambassadors who try to intervene in our country and yet know so little about our people, culture, and language?

68. Aren't most of the Americans we see in our country—businesspeople, missionaries, Peace Corps volunteers, etc.—involved in intelligence gathering for the CIA?

69. Why does your country participate in the training of military dictators?

70. Given the fact that the majority of world resources are consumed by developed countries and these countries are responsible for major global environmental degradation, what is the U.S. government doing to preserve the global environment? What is it doing to clean up the environmental mess in areas such as eastern Europe and Latin America?

PREFACE

In 1983, Charles T. Vetter Jr.—a consultant, lecturer, and former senior executive training officer with the U.S. Department of State's Foreign Service Institute—authored *Citizen Ambassadors: Guidelines to Responding to Questions Asked about America.* Vetter's intent was to provide sample responses to questions he had encountered throughout his decades of experience conversing with non-Americans. He illustrated, through those responses, the attitudes and approaches he had found most effective. In fact, Vetter stressed that our attitude can ofttimes be more important than the information we convey in our conversations with international visitors or acquaintances. The principles behind Vetter's 1983 publication are still central to this publication. What has changed is the information. The Kennedy Center has updated *Citizen Ambassadors* to reflect the dramatic cultural, political, and economic changes that have taken place since the end of the Cold War. The result: *Citizen Diplomacy: Responding to Questions about America.*

One reviewer said, "*Citizen Diplomacy* should be required reading for all students traveling outside the United States." We agree. *Citizen Diplomacy* is primarily intended for those who travel abroad or host international visitors in the United States—Americans who find themselves in the position of a citizen diplomat. However, even visitors from outside the United States will likely find much in the book enlightening. Like its predecessor, *Citizen Ambassadors*, *Citizen Diplomacy* contains a collection of commonly asked questions about the United States. It also contains sample responses; however, *Citizen Diplomacy* is not an official handbook offering definitive, immutable answers. Hopefully, readers will find the information helpful in formulating their replies to questions posed to them, but again, the style of the responses—balanced, nonconfrontational, and nondefensive—may be more important than their content.

The general introduction (page 1) and chapter introductions were prepared by Robert R. King, minority staff director of the Subcommittee on International Operations and Human Rights of the Committee on International Relations, U.S. House of Representatives; and chief-of-staff to Congressman Tom Lantos of California. King holds a Ph.D. from the Fletcher School of Law and Diplomacy.

As with *Citizen Ambassadors* before it, *Citizen Diplomacy* required a team effort. Many individuals shared their insights and suggestions, helping to produce a valuable tool for building productive, meaningful intercultural relationships. However, all successful efforts require a leader, someone who will see the job through to the finish. Amy Lynn Andrus, an associate editor in the publications division of the David M. Kennedy Center for International Studies, shepherded *Citizen Diplomacy*. With steady zeal and unrelenting persistence, Amy correlated, researched, and crafted a stellar manuscript. We appreciate her exemplary effort.

Greg Adams, Thomas G. Alexander, Rodney B. Boynton, R. Lanier Britsch, Joseph A. Cannon, Richard H. Cracroft, David C. Deem, Jessie L. Embry, Jeannie Evans, Mark R. Grandstaff, John R. Hughes, Ruki Jayaraman, Kerk L. Phillips, Jeffrey F. Ringer, Jordan Tanner, Stan A. Taylor, V. Lynn Tyler, and Charles T. Vetter Jr. provided meaningful assistance throughout the updating process. We thank them. In addition, we acknowledge the invaluable feedback and support of the members of the Kennedy Center Publications Committee.

Finally, we recognize the design expertise of Matt Scherer and photography talent of John Rees in creating *Citizen Diplomacy's* stunning cover.

GRANT PAUL SKABELUND
Managing Editor
October 1995

INTRODUCTION

INTRODUCTION

INCREASING INTERNATIONAL CONTACTS:
LIVING IN A SHRINKING WORLD

This book is for Americans who travel abroad for business or pleasure and for Americans who come into contact with international visitors in the United States.[1] That constitutes a broad audience because Americans are dealing with non-Americans in ever greater numbers. Whatever their occupation or position in life, Americans increasingly encounter non-Americans from a variety of other countries and cultures—on travels abroad, in business or leisure activities at home, in social encounters, and in chance meetings.

The speed, convenience, and relative decline in the cost of international travel have all contributed to an exponential increase in international contacts over the past half century. Travel by Americans and travel to America have never been more common. Statistics indicate the extent of expanding international contact. It was predicted that in 1995 the number of international visitors arriving in the United States would exceed fifty-one million; for most of the previous decade, international travel to the U.S. increased at an average annual rate of more than 8 percent.[2]

---

1. *Americans* is a convenient, shorthand way of referring to citizens and residents of the United States. The term is used throughout this book, without the intent of overlooking the fact that there are other *Americans* who live in North, Central, and South America.

2. U.S. Travel and Tourism Administration (USTTA) forecast, cited in U.S. Department of Commerce, "Table 1: Origin of International Visitors to United States, 1992–1995," in *U.S. Industrial Outlook 1994*, 35th ed. (Wash., D.C.: Government Printing Office, 1994), 41–4; see also 41–3.

Some of these numbers clearly represent the same individuals visiting more than once during the year; nevertheless, the sheer number of visitors to the United States is remarkable.

Travel to the United States has increased substantially during this century. In 1930, the last year before the Great Depression reduced travel substantially, the number of non-American travelers who arrived in the United States by air or sea reached 346,183. In 1950, when international travel was on the rebound following the end of World War II, there were 530,209 non-U.S. international arrivals in the United States. By 1970, that number had increased to 3,831,200.[3] Since then it has increased more than twelve-fold.[4]

International travel by Americans has likewise grown substantially over the years. Predictions indicated that in 1994 nearly fifty million U.S. residents would leave our country for foreign destinations.[5] The number of Americans who travel abroad fluctuates because of economic downturns and international crises (travel was down significantly in 1991 and 1992 as a result of the U.S. recession and concerns about terrorism during and after the Persian Gulf War), but overall the number of Americans traveling has increased substantially. In 1930, some 445,485 U.S. citizens left for foreign destinations by air and sea. By 1950, that number had grown to 651,595, and by 1970, it had increased nearly ten-fold to 6,107,257.[6]

Over the years, there have been important shifts in international visitors' countries of origin and in the countries Americans visit. In 1931, 65 percent of U.S. citizens and noncitizens arriving in the United States

---

3. U.S. Bureau of the Census, "Series C 296–301. Passenger Arrivals and Departures: 1908 to 1970," in *Historical Statistics of the United States: Colonial Times to 1970*, part 1 (Wash., D.C.: Government Printing Office, 1975), 119.

4. USTTA projection, cited in U.S. Bureau of the Census, "Table No. 421. Foreign Travel to the United States, With Projections: 1985 to 1994," in *Statistical Abstract of the United States: 1994*, 114th ed. (Wash., D.C.: Government Printing Office, 1994), 265.

5. USTTA projection, cited in U.S. Bureau of the Census, "Table No. 420: U.S. Travel to Foreign Countries, With Projections: 1985 to 1994," in *Statistical Abstract*, 264.

6. U.S. Bureau of the Census, "Series C 296–301."

by air and sea were from Europe. By 1970, international arrivals by air and sea from Europe had declined to just over 40 percent.[7] Forecasts indicated that in 1995 only 21 percent of visitors would be from European countries, 12 percent from Asia, and a full 6 percent from Central and South America. Predictions indicated further that a substantial portion of the visitors to the United States in 1995 would come from its nearest neighbors: seventeen million arrivals from Canada (34 percent) and eleven million from Mexico (22 percent).[8]

The destinations of Americans traveling abroad are similar. Mexico is the most popular destination by far, with sixteen-million-plus Americans (some 37 percent of travel abroad by U.S. citizens) visiting Mexico in 1992. Canada is the second most popular destination with almost twelve million American visitors in 1992 (27 percent of American trips abroad). European countries received some 16 percent of American visitors, and Central and South America received 12 percent. The remaining 8 percent traveled to Asia, Africa, and Australia.[9]

Non-Americans have a keen interest in the United States. They travel to America to see the country and to meet and understand its people. Those we meet when we travel abroad are similarly curious. People everywhere are acutely aware of American influence, simply because of the size of the U.S. economy, America's global military and diplomatic presence, the worldwide scope of U.S. national interests, and the impact of American culture (i.e., movies, television, sports, popular music, fashions, and art). Around the world people use Visa or MasterCard, "boot up" their computers with MS–DOS so that they can use WordPerfect in English or in numerous other languages, fly in Boeing aircraft, put Exxon gasoline in their automobiles, wear Levis, and eat at McDonald's from Moscow to Manila and from Madrid to Melbourne. The worldwide

---

7. U.S. Bureau of the Census, "Series C 302–316. Passengers Arriving, by Area of Embarkation, Flag of Carrier, and Mode of Travel: 1931–1970," in *Historical Statistics*, 119–20.

8. USTTA forecast, cited in U.S. Department of Commerce, "Table 1."

9. USTTA statistic, cited in U.S. Bureau of the Census, "Table No. 420."

expansion of the computer Internet will likely only increase the pace at which American culture is transported abroad.

Because of its size and the far-reaching influence of its culture, politics, and business, the United States has a global impact. Citizens of most other countries are aware of this impact on their lives. In contrast, Americans are considerably less aware of other cultures and events in other countries. To some extent this is natural: generally speaking, developments in the United States have a much greater impact beyond our borders than events abroad have on us. Americans are not necessarily hostile to other countries and cultures; some are simply not aware, while others are just not interested.

As a result, many non-Americans have something of a love-hate attitude toward the United States and Americans. On one hand, there is an international respect and fascination with things American, but on the other, there is resentment and frustration concerning the United States's influence and policies, the negative aspects of American cultural influence, and the seeming indifference Americans exhibit toward others.

As we meet non-Americans abroad and at home, we are representatives of the United States, whether we wish to be or not. Our presence will elicit questions about the United States—about what non-Americans consider to be its positive *and* its negative aspects. How we respond to such questions makes an important difference, not only in our intercultural, interpersonal relations but in people's attitudes toward America, the country, as well. Therefore, we are all "citizen diplomats."

CITIZEN DIPLOMACY AS A TOOL

This book can help you in your role of citizen diplomat as you seek to respond to questions from visitors here or from your hosts when you are the visitor abroad. *Citizen Diplomacy* can be used in at least two ways: as an easy reference for answers or as a complete text. If you need a quick response to a question, scan the "List of Questions," beginning on page vii, find a question similar to the one you are responding to, and look up the sample response given. The list is organized by topic:

- Chapter One: American Society and Culture
- Chapter Two: American Government
- Chapter Three: America in the World Economy
- Chapter Four: American Foreign Policy

However, you may first want to read the book as a text. The general introduction, guidelines, and chapter introductions will help you build the theoretical and practical foundations needed to respond to questions with consistency and sensitivity. At the very least, review the "Guidelines for Formulating Responses" below, which served as a basis for all of the sample responses contained in *Citizen Diplomacy*. Studying and internalizing the guidelines will help you to better "think on your feet" as you formulate your own responses to questions about America.

Frequently you will encounter friendly inquiries from individuals simply seeking information or wanting to understand why or how things are done in America. Other times, however, you will find that questions can be hostile. No nation with the international influence America has exercised, particularly since World War II, can generate universally positive responses. U.S. policies in some cases have been hostile to particular governments, and many elements of American culture are not universally welcomed abroad.

Based on the experiences of a number of well-traveled Americans, the questions in this volume are some of the most commonly asked questions you are likely to encounter. The sample responses are thoughtful and balanced, and they seek to provide the amount of information and level of detail appropriate for most international visitors. But they are only *sample* responses; they are not definitive. In all cases considerably more—or very different—information could be provided.[10] You may be able to give better, more detailed responses to some of these questions

---

10. The responses attempt to offer broad, fair descriptions of the feelings and views of "Americans"—in general. Of course, the term *Americans* covers an extremely diverse group of individuals with diverse opinions. Given obvious space limitations, however, the complete spectrum of Americans' feelings and opinions could not be represented in every sample response.

than those presented here. Depending on the type of information your questioner is seeking, you may want to formulate a response based on your personal opinions (see page 10). Caution is in order, however. It is important to gauge whether your fellow interlocutor is seeking to sample a few light *hors d'oeuvres* or whether he or she is interested in delving into the *entrée* with knife and fork. Do not hesitate to go beyond the information given in these sample responses if you have good reason to do so. You and your questioner may share the same academic specialization or a similar business background that provides common ground for dealing with certain topics in greater depth.

The carefully balanced, nondefensive tone of the responses included in this book is their most important attribute. In a great many cases, the tone and style of the response—the attitude conveyed therein—is far more important than the specific facts communicated. The responses here provide good information, but they are equally useful in giving you the sense of balance that ought to be conveyed when responding to questions.

The following are more specific guidelines for developing citizen diplomacy skills—for developing a balanced, nondefensive, nonconfrontational, and effective style in responding to questions about America.

DEVELOPING CITIZEN DIPLOMACY SKILLS:
GUIDELINES FOR FORMULATING RESPONSES

Avoid defensiveness: Consider the source

You may find yourself getting defensive because questions about America often deal with stereotypes and are phrased in a direct or even blunt manner:

Italian national: *"Why don't Americans choose more intelligent presidents?"*
Defensive American: *"Well, at least we don't vote for fascists."*

Resist any temptation to lash out. The injunction in Proverbs is always appropriate when responding to questions: "A soft answer turneth away wrath: but grievous words stir up anger."[11] It is best to keep your ego from becoming involved in the response. While you may feel your opinion is obviously superior to the "fuzzy-headed" thinking of the "dolts" who disagree with you, a response that conveys such an attitude may be less appealing to another person.

Keep in mind that, just as we have limited information about other peoples and their countries, non-Americans may have access to limited or distorted information about America, and such information often leads to thinking in stereotypes. You may want to say politely, "That's an interesting question. Where did you learn that?" Knowing the source of information can give you additional insight into how a question might be addressed or a misconception cleared up.

Often generalizations made by international acquaintances contain a grain of truth but are not completely true. Rather than defensively attacking what is untrue, begin by accepting what could be true. Then try to clear up any misunderstandings your acquaintance may have. In attempting to avoid defensiveness, remember that balance remains an important element of any response. Oftentimes, the questions you field will relate to what others see as negative aspects of American society or government. To avoid coming across as defensive, you may bend over backwards, conceding all of the negative points a questioner brings up. Conceding such points, if they are valid, is fine; you should strive to present an honest picture of the state of American society. But at the same time, make questioners aware of those steps our government and fellow citizens are taking to ameliorate and overcome our problems.

Remember that inquirers may have limited English skills. The phrasing of their questions, therefore, may not convey the subtleties of their thoughts; queries may come across as brusque, tactless, and even offensive. Try to "read between the lines" and suspend judgment on your

---

11. Proverbs 15:1.

questioners' intent. You may find it useful to repeat the question or comment to verify that you have correctly understood its meaning.

Consider your questioners' motivation

Suspending judgment may help you treat each question as if it were sincere. If queries seem hostile or critical and you respond facetiously or in a sarcastic or negative tone, you could automatically cut off a channel of desirable communication. In conversation, people may mirror your attitude. So if you are sincere, friendly, open, and respectful, they will most likely reciprocate, even if you do not reach agreement on an issue.

While this seems like conflicting advice, you may also want to probe for questioners' motives. Are they asking this question out of curiosity? to increase understanding? to enter into an intellectual and cultural debate? to display their knowledge?

Some may have been asked similar questions and feel a need to find appropriate responses for others, as well as for themselves. However, some may simply want to spar verbally or play an intellectual game—not to be enlightened. They may already have a fixed opinion and just want to see how you react. In these cases, trying to sense their motivation can save you a lot of frustration. Simply present your point. Do not argue or try to win over your audience. Citizen diplomacy often requires forbearance.

Consider your knowledge and opinions

Most people are looking for a *balanced*, factual answer based on your knowledge of the subject. They want to see the big picture—to see the different views Americans hold on important issues. In fact, there is a broad diversity of views among Americans on most issues, and it is generally better to discuss the range of opinions and provide a balanced assessment of those views, with some reflection on the reasons for the differences, rather than argue a particular position. A general explanation of differing views can be more illuminating than a detailed response presenting only one opinion.

Still, some may want the more personal opinion of someone who has actually "been there, seen it, and done it," as well. They might consider your personal experiences and opinions to be your most credible and interesting sources of information. Include your personal opinion if solicited; just be sure to identify opinion as opinion and not fact.

If you don't have a personal opinion on a given topic, don't be fearful of admitting that you don't. Proclaiming your neutrality on an issue and then being open to counsel may be the best approach in some cases.

When asked a question on a topic about which you have limited or no knowledge, you may be embarrassed and feel defensive. However, saying "I didn't come here to talk about that" or repeatedly saying "I don't know" could, justifiably, be considered rude. If you have insufficient knowledge or experience to offer an acceptable response, be honest. Let the questioner know that you have a limited perspective and are not an expert on the subject. Possible approaches to responding to such questions include

"My experience has been . . . "
"My personal feeling is . . . "
"I'm no expert, but my own impression is . . . "
"Other Americans may have different opinions, but . . . ."

Attempting to respond to a question, even when you feel inadequate, conveys to questioners that you are genuinely interested in them and their feelings.

If you don't have the knowledge to respond to the original question, the questioner may have an underlying concern that you *can* address. Again, try to read between the lines and draw out hidden concerns. In addition, questions may require factual information that you simply cannot quote from memory. If you have the time and inclination, tell questioners that you are willing to help them find the information they are seeking. And then follow up. The epilogue contains information on sources that you might find helpful in researching certain topics (see page 204).

Consider your audience

In the process of formulating and articulating responses, keep your audience in mind. Try to understand the point of view of the individuals raising questions. What are the national and international concerns and interests of their country? What is the state of relations of that country with the United States, and how have our two countries agreed or disagreed on recent international issues? Considering the individuals' religious, cultural, socioeconomic, and educational backgrounds can also help you phrase your answer in an understandable, inoffensive way. You may be able to compare and contrast their country's culture, political situation, or other characteristics with yours and, thus, make your response more comprehensible. (However, you will want to avoid making negative and unflattering comparisons between the United States and their country.)

Obviously the answers contained in this book are written for a very general audience. As you read through them, remember that you will likely want to customize your response to fit the culture and background of your specific audience.

Many of the responses in this book contain words and phrases that could be too complicated for nonnative English speakers. You will probably need to "translate" your answers into more basic English than you are accustomed to speaking or writing. Avoid slang words and colloquial phrases. Use common words. And if you are familiar with the listener's native language, use simple English cognates. For example, native Spanish speakers with limited English skills are more likely to understand *impossible* than *inconceivable* because it is closer to the Spanish word *imposible*. In addition, avoid quotes, literary examples, jokes, abbreviations, events, people, or other references with which your audience may not be familiar; such references will confuse, rather than enhance, the conversation.

Remember to speak clearly, slowly, and enunciate. Do not slur words together (people will understand "Let's go to lunch" more easily than "Let's gulunch"), and do not speak more loudly than necessary. Speaking loudly does not ensure understanding and may insult your listener. On the other hand, making sure that nonnative English speakers can see your lips when you talk *will* increase their comprehension.

Cross-cultural interaction skills are not limited to responding to questions comprehensibly. Other skills include knowing when to laugh or even smile, how to stand and how close to stand to your questioner, what questions to ask and how, and even when to make eye contact. Finding out more about the cultural mores of your audience will help you effectively relate to your audience in manner, as well as in word. The epilogue discusses some resources on culture and intercultural communication that will help you learn more about relating to your specific audience (see page 204).

Invite questions

Some may be embarrassed and hesitant to ask questions of a foreigner. They may feel that asking questions is inappropriate, impolite, and too confrontational. Or they may not want to display their "ignorance" of U.S. culture. Be aware, too, that cultural limits on interaction between people of different ages, sex, or social status may preclude someone from addressing you directly. However, in most cases you can make it easier for someone who is curious about America but simply does not know how to broach the subject.

You can invite questions by offering potential questioners an opening. You might comment that you heard something about their country and would like to know if it were true or could be clarified. This demonstrates a desire on your part to understand their country and opens the door for a conversation about culture. With the door open, they may feel more comfortable responding in kind with a question about the United States. You might also ask them how they feel about controversial U.S. actions or policies as they affect the world or their country. Such a question demonstrates that you are not embarrassed to talk openly about the United States—even about what some consider to be its shortcomings.

Of course, in initiating a conversation you should always keep in mind which topics of conversation are deemed appropriate in that culture, where they are appropriate, and when they are appropriate. If you question the suitability of a certain subject, do not bring it up. Again, being observant and studying materials on cultural mores should help you determine what constitutes appropriate topics of conversation (see page 204 for more information).

There are few, if any, pat answers or approaches. The specific responses you give will depend on the situation, your audience, and your personal experience, opinions, and knowledge. Practice with intercultural materials and, most importantly, in real-life situations will help you determine the best approach and most understandable response to use in a given situation.

We are blessed with a fascinating country and interesting fellow citizens. Discussing America and Americans can be a delightful experience. The interest of others in our insight is flattering, and as we think about the questions posed to us and explore responses with others who have a different point of view, we develop an increased understanding of our country. Furthermore, thinking about how others see us, as Americans, can help us better understand ourselves. We are all citizen diplomats. Taking that responsibility seriously can make our interactions with those living abroad and with international visitors in the United States more interesting, meaningful, and enlightening. Ultimately, it can also help build bridges of understanding between peoples and cultures.

ROBERT R. KING
McLean, Virginia
October 1995

CHAPTER ONE

ONE

AMERICAN CULTURE AND SOCIETY

American society and culture are surprisingly visible virtually throughout the world. American movies and television programs are intensely
watched from Paris, France (where they are observed with considerable
apprehension, at least by cultural bureaucrats and intellectuals who fear
the inundation of French culture by American culture), to Phnom Penh,
Cambodia (where American culture is spread through pirated editions
of U.S. software programs, designer clothes, popular music recordings,
and movies, with little regard for international copyright laws).

The pervasiveness of American movies and television programs gives
non-Americans extensive exposure to American life. American producers routinely consider the international market in their financial calcula-
tions when creating new movies and television programs. Overall, international sales of American movies and programs generate 80 percent of
the income they gross in the domestic American market, and some films
generate considerably more abroad than they do at home.[1] The astronomical fees paid to such actors as Sylvester Stallone, Arnold
Schwarzenegger, and Bruce Willis reflect the substantial appeal action

---

1. Standard & Poor's Corporation, "Box Office Reaches Record Level," in *Standard & Poor's Industry Surveys*, vol. 1 (April 1995): L21–L22.

heroes hold for non-American audiences. The attention devoted to international sales of American films and recordings, which appear in the latest issues of *Variety* or *Billboard*, indicates how ubiquitous products of the American entertainment industry are internationally and how important the non-American audience is to American "culture" moguls.

We live in an age in which the society and culture of the United States increasingly dominates international culture. Our popular musicians define the style and set the pace for youth culture. French, Russian, and Filipino pop musicians sing in English. Occasionally, non-American groups generate broad interest in the United States, but as the British Beatles found out in the 1960s, success in the American market is generally key to international success.

One of the problems with our international cultural influence, however, is that what non-Americans see is generally not the best of our culture. Action, adventure, crime, and violence generate much greater interest with international movie audiences than do tamer topics—just as they do with American audiences. According to one writer, French children are so accustomed to American crime movies and television programs that, if ever arrested, they expect to be told "you have the right to remain silent," as guaranteed under U.S. law.[2]

One example of the distorted picture that is sometimes conveyed through television and movies is the image of America Polish audiences saw on their domestic television broadcasts in the 1970s. The TV series *Kojak* was the only major American television program that was regularly broadcast in Poland. Polish television purchased the series for display because (1) the hero was a Polish American, which gave Poles an immediate interest and link with the story; (2) it was politically acceptable to the communist ideological watchdogs because it showed the seamy side of America (Kojak was constantly dealing with crime, drugs, prostitution, and violence); (3) action programs like *Kojak* translate relatively

---

2. Diana Quintero, "American Television and Cinema in France and Europe," *Fletcher Forum of World Affairs* 18, no. 2 (summer/fall 1994): 118.

easily into another language because the action is easy to follow and the dialogue is not complex; and (4) the *Kojak* series was available at a price that the Poles could afford to pay. The result was that Polish audiences had a *Kojak*-centered image of the United States. While Poland in the 1970s is a particularly dramatic example, the situation is similar today. The image of America shown in our movies and television programs does not give a multifaceted picture of the complexities of American life.

The first point to keep in mind when answering questions about our society, culture, and way of life is that your questioners will feel they know something about the United States based on their exposure to American movies, television programs, and popular music. This is true even if they are visiting the United States for the first time or have never even left their homeland. In many regards, non-Americans' sense of familiarity with American culture and society makes responding to their questions more difficult. The non-Americans we meet already have certain preconceptions about U.S. life based on their exposure to U.S. popular culture, but unfortunately, many of these perceptions are widely inaccurate and distorted. American movies, television programs, and popular music as a whole are hardly representative of the complex totality of the United States's national culture and society, but the smaller spectrum of the entertainment media that is popular abroad gives an even more one-sided and distorted picture of American life. In answering questions, keep in mind that, while we understand the entertainment media gives a distorted view of our society, non-Americans may not understand this distortion. The assumptions about the media that we take for granted most likely will need to be explained and made explicit in your conversations with non-Americans.

A second element to keep in mind is that America is a particularly diverse society.[3] Most foreign visitors to the United States have experience with a culture and society that is considerably more homogeneous

---

3. For a discussion of how America's diversity affects political behavior, see chapter 2, particularly questions 23, 27, 32, 33, 34, 36, and 37.

than the United States's. Migration flows and urbanization have contributed to substantial social change in industrialized and developing countries alike, but for the most part other countries have more unified and coherent societies. Rather than having a historic culture that has evolved over centuries, American culture is a recent phenomenon, with a number of diverse and contradictory strands. In addition to the English and northern European traditions that traditionally were considered to form the basis of American culture, Native American, African, southern and eastern European, Hispanic, and Asian influences have contributed to the richness, diversity, and complexity of the nation's culture.

A third consideration is that American society is presently going through a period of major cultural, social, and economic change. The 1990 census reflected some of the scope of this ongoing transformation. In 1990, the foreign-born portion of the U.S. population was 8 percent or nearly twenty million people—the highest number since such statistics have been kept by the federal government. This is an even higher number than was found in the United States during the early decades of this century when massive waves of immigrants entered the country, prompting severe restrictions on immigration.[4] From 1990 to 1995, the number of immigrants entering the United States has averaged almost one million per year; this figure is the highest since the turn of the century. Over the next decade immigration will continue, and America's population growth will be increasingly due to new arrivals.[5]

One consequence of this nonnative population growth is the rise of antiforeign sentiment. Furthermore, much of this migrant influx is non-

4. U.S. Bureau of the Census, "Series C 228–295. Foreign-Born Population, by Country of Birth: 1850 to 1970," in *Historical Statistics of the United States: Colonial Times to 1970*, part 1 (Wash., D.C.: Government Printing Office, 1975), 117; U.S. Bureau of the Census, "Table No. 54. Native and Foreign-Born Population, by Place of Birth: 1920 to 1990," in *Statistical Abstract of the United States: 1994*, 114th ed. (Wash., D.C.: Government Printing Office, 1994), 52.

5. Peter Francese, "America at Mid-Decade," *American Demographics* 17, no. 2 (February 1995): 26–27

European and nonwhite. As a result of nonwhite migration and higher birth rates among Hispanics, African Americans, and Asians, the "minority" segment of the American population is growing at a faster rate than the white population. If these present trends continue, California will have a nonwhite majority by the end of the 1990s, and minorities will make up one-half of the total population of the United States by the middle of the next century.[6]

American family life is also not as homogenous as some might think. The "all-American" family—a married couple with children—continues to shrink as a portion of our population. In 1995, only a bare majority of U.S. households were composed of married couples living together, and only about one-third of the total had children under the age of eighteen. The share of families with children living at home will continue to decline. Furthermore, America, which has promoted the glorification of youth, has a population that is graying. As the "baby boomers" born in the post-World War II years age, the middle-aged segment of our population is the fastest growing, but over the next decade or two, the elderly population will grow even faster.[7]

Where Americans live is also changing. One-half century ago, New York was the largest state in population, and the Chicago-to-Boston corridor was the most densely populated area of the country. Now New York is the third most populous state and is quickly loosing ground as the population shifts south and west. California is the largest U.S. state; with about thirty-two million people it is larger than over half the countries that are members of the United Nations. Texas has replaced New York as the second largest state, and Florida, whose population grew

---

6. The information in this paragraph is based on the following sources: Rochelle L. Stanfield, "Strains in the Family," *National Journal* 23, no. 39 (28 September 1991): 2318–19; Gabrielle Sándor, "The 'Other' Americans," *American Demographics* 16, no. 6 (June 1994): 38.

7. The information in this paragraph is based on the following sources: The Editors, "The Future of Households," *American Demographics* 15, no. 12 (December 1993): 29; Francese, "America at Mid-Decade," 24.

more than 9 percent during the past five years, will likely pass New York not long after the turn of the millennium.[8]

The integration of the United States into a global economy has also contributed to social changes. Jobs in the manufacturing sector, which tend to be relatively better paid, have declined over the past quarter century, while typically lower-paying jobs in the service sector—particularly in health-care and social services—have increased. Global competition has led to corporate downsizing and economic uncertainties that have pressed the middle class. These changes are reflected in economic statistics: from the 1970s to the 1990s, the combined household income of the middle 60 percent of households shrunk from 52 to 48 percent of total household income. Meanwhile, the share of income going to the top 20 percent of households has increased from 44 to 48 percent of total household income.[9]

Furthermore, the social changes that are taking place have altered some of the stereotypes of Americans in the minds of non-Americans; at the same time, Americans still think of ourselves in a traditional light, in some respects. The political rhetoric about "family values" is very much a reflection of what we would like to think about the nature of America and ourselves. However, the social and cultural features that are most dominant in the minds of non-Americans are based on information they receive from the American media, are cultural elements that are not family-values oriented, and in truth, are not part of most Americans' direct experience. Thus, how we think of ourselves and how others think of us tend to emphasize opposite elements.

In short, American culture and society is changing due to a number of factors. Being aware of, interpreting, and describing that change can be simultaneously a challenge and a service in our communications with non-Americans.

---

8. The information in this paragraph is based on the following sources: Francese, "America at Mid-Decade," 28; U.S. Bureau of the Census, "State Rankings" and "Table No. 34. State Population Projections: 1995 to 2010," in *Statistical Abstract*, xii, 33.

9. Francese, "America at Mid-Decade," 25, 29.

1 : *What are the respective roles of American women and men? What is the relationship between American men and women like? To people in my country, American women seem very "aggressive."*

A variety of economic and social movements has greatly affected American men's and women's roles over the years.[10] Over a century ago, in agricultural America, men and women often worked in the fields side by side, and the work women did in the home was considered an economic necessity. It kept the family enterprise running and financially stable. With industrialization came a greater distinction between work and home. "Real work" became an activity that earned a paycheck and was on a strict timetable; thus the economic merit of housework, which was largely performed by women, was devalued.

Another phenomenon that changed men's and women's roles was the redefinition of children's roles. With the enactment of national child labor laws in the early 1900s, a child's place was at school or home, not in the workplace. It became the responsibility of women to stay at home with the children, nurture them through childhood and adolescence, and create a pleasant home environment that their husbands could enjoy after a day's work. The man's responsibility was to provide an adequate income to sustain his wife and children. Men's and women's very natures were considered well suited to such roles: men were considered aggressive and ambitious, while women were nurturing, caring, and "unfit" for the rough world of industry and business. The ideal was a marked division of labor between the sexes. For the majority of Americans, domestic work was feminine. "Formal" work was masculine.

---

10. The following served as general sources for the information contained in this response: Tamara K. Hareven, "Continuity and Change in American Family Life," in *Making America: The Society & Culture of the United States*, ed. Luther S. Luedtke (Chapel Hill: University of North Carolina Press, 1992), 308–26; William H. Chafe, "Women and American Society," in *Making America*, 327–40.

Throughout the twentieth century, men's roles have remained the same to an extent: men are still expected to be a family provider. However, women's roles have changed dramatically, and men, in many ways, have been expected simply to "adjust."

At the end of the nineteenth and beginning of the twentieth century, women began creating organizations dedicated to social change and women's rights. Perhaps their most notable success was gaining for women the right to vote in 1920. World War II also affected the status of women; more women entered the formal workforce due to the shortage of male workers and the labor demand of defense and other industries. When American men returned from war, women were urged by employers, the government, and the media to relinquish their jobs to returning soldiers. Polls showed, however, that the vast majority of American women who held jobs would have preferred to retain them. [11]

After World War II, domestic work for women was reemphasized and portrayed in the media as the norm. However, the separate roles of men and women were harder to maintain than before. Families found obtaining the post-war ideal of a home, car, appliances, television, and other amenities difficult on one man's income. And women who had enjoyed working outside the home during wartime wanted to return to the formal workplace.

The civil rights movement of the 1950s and 1960s—generally associated with racial equality—gave Americans the opportunity to work toward more equitable male and female roles. Members of a variety of organizations expressed frustration and anger at the lack of equal opportunities and rights for American women, particularly in the formal workplace. Eventually, the Civil Rights Act (1964) prohibited job discrimination based on sex. Many feminists demanded an equal rights constitutional amendment, which failed to become law. However, the feminist movement continued and has had far-reaching and profound consequences.

---

11. Chafe, "Women and American Society," 330–31.

All of these social and economic movements have had a large impact on the majority of the population. Americans are constantly adjusting to their roles as women and men because these roles are constantly being redefined. Changing gender roles affect every aspect of American society: individual relationships, family relationships, politics, education, business, and religion.

Generally speaking, in gender relationships, American men and women increasingly regard each other as equals. American women have more opportunities for education, more legal rights, more alternatives, and more economic power than ever before; therefore, they are more likely to resist any perceived attempts of men to "control" them or make their decisions. Non-Americans may interpret this behavior as "aggressive," but American women consider controlling their lives and acting independently as their right.

Whether women want to work or have to work out of economic necessity, more and more women are competing for jobs with men and are demanding equal pay for equal work. Again, some may interpret this as aggressive behavior. Women are also working in fields that have traditionally been dominated by men. The number of Ph.D.s among American women tripled between 1970 and 1990.[12] And women increasingly work as business executives, lawyers, politicians, architects, doctors, pilots, firefighters—even ministers. Even so, studies show that a "glass ceiling" exists for many women in the workplace. Discrimination, though illegal, still keeps some women from being promoted and reaching top positions, in proportion to their representation, in many professions. American men have had to adjust to the influx of women in the workplace—in relating to women as coworkers and colleagues and not just as mothers, sisters, and wives.

Between 1970 and the early 1990s, the percentage of married women in the workforce increased from just over 40 percent to nearly 60 per-

---

12. Ibid., 334.

cent.[13] Thus, men have had to adjust to their spouses working as well. Working women have less time to do housework and care for their children than women one or two generations ago. Some husbands and wives rely on day care. Others choose not to have children. A small proportion of men stay home with the children while their wives work. Increasingly men are expected to help more at home after work—more than their fathers and grandfathers did—fixing meals, doing housework, and tending the children. The ideal, though many couples have yet to achieve it, is an equal partnership at home between men and women.

Certainly, the United States is not the only country that has experienced dramatic changes in the roles of men and women. All countries will continue to experience economic forces and social movements that challenge customary gender roles.

Related information: questions 2, 32

2 : *We hear so much about the disintegration of the American family. Is divorce the cause?*

Before the age of modern medicine, American parents and grandparents often died at a younger age; thus "nuclear" families (two generations living in a household) and even one-parent families were not uncommon.[14] In addition, immigrants to the United States—who varied in their social, ethnic, religious, and economic backgrounds—brought different family traditions and structures with them. So the American family has always been somewhat structurally diverse. However, by the mid-twentieth century, 80 percent of American children lived with both biological parents through childhood. By 1980, this trend was reversed;

---

13. U.S. Bureau of Labor statistic, cited in *Time Almanac*, 1994 CD-ROM reference ed., s.v. "Labor Force Participation Rates, by Marital Status, Sex, & Age: 1970–1992."

14. The following served as general sources for the information contained in this response: Hareven, "Continuity and Change"; Barbara Dafoe Whitehead, "Dan Quayle Was Right," *Atlantic Monthly* 271, no. 4 (April 1993): 47–84.

only 50 percent of American children were living with both of their parents through childhood.[15]

Change in the "traditional family" structure that was prevalent fifty years ago has come about for a variety of reasons. The 1960s and 1970s brought several social movements that transformed traditional roles and values. Most notable, perhaps, is the sexual revolution, which was accompanied by messages of sexual freedom and personal gratification. These messages radically changed many Americans' behavior. The idea of sexual "freedom" and the increasing availability and convenience of contraception contributed to the increase of teenage and premarital sex. Much of the American media began portraying premarital and teenage sex as normal—even glamorous. Today, the media has been increasingly criticized for not also portraying the consequences of such behavior, such as sexually transmitted diseases (including AIDS) and teenage pregnancy.

Whether because of media messages, lack of education, or carelessness, many teenagers and adults now engage in sexual activity without using contraception. Hence, procreation is no longer reserved for marriage, and single parenthood does not carry the social stigma it once did. During the mid-twentieth century, only 5 percent of children were born out of wedlock.[16] By 1992, the number had jumped to 30 percent.[17] Though most teen pregnancies are unplanned, some teenage girls want to get pregnant, believing that pregnancy will gain them attention, will lead to marriage and stability, or that a child will be a new source of love and acceptance. Urban economic problems also contribute to increasing rates of single parenthood. Some inner-city men are unable to find or keep jobs that lead to a stable income and, therefore, may father children without intending or being able to support them. However, single parenthood is not a social trend unique to the urban poor.

---

15. Whitehead, "Quayle Was Right," 47.

16. Ibid., 50.

17. National Center for Health Statistics, cited in Tamar Lewin, "Births to Young Teen-Agers Decline, Agency Says," *New York Times*, 26 October 1994, late edition, sec. A.

Divorce has certainly changed the structure of the American family. Between the 1950s and 1990s, the divorce rate in America more than doubled due to a number of factors.[18] As American society began to value individual freedom over family stability, the stigma of divorce decreased; divorce was seen as a way for adults to gain independence and pursue their individual desires. The women's movement also created greater opportunities for and acceptance of women in the formal workforce, which made women less financially dependent on men. They no longer had to rely on the institution of marriage to provide economic stability, and thus, divorce became a viable option for them. Even America's churches (with the notable exception of the Catholic Church) no longer forbade divorce. Certainly greater social acceptance of divorce allowed many Americans to escape unhappy marriages, some involving serious mental and physical abuse. But divorce has also become something of a "quick fix"—a way for men and women to find instant release from the pressures that accompany married life in today's complex and stressful society.

Other less traditional family forms have multiplied over the last fifty years. Increased single parenthood and divorce have resulted in more American stepfamilies than ever before. In addition, more Americans are cohabiting, in heterosexual or homosexual relationships. Statistically, stepfamilies and live-in relationships are more unstable than traditional marriages.

Of course traditional families, with two biological, married parents, face challenges as well. Several factors have led to less family cohesion and interaction than in past generations. Whether because of economic need or personal desire, both parents in many families work in the formal workplace, thus decreasing family interaction time. Therefore, television, other forms of entertainment, and peers typically play a larger role in children's lives than they did several decades ago. The stresses and hectic schedules accompanying modern life can also decrease family interaction.

---

18. Whitehead, "Quayle Was Right," 50.

Many of the changes in American mores and the American family structure may have benefited adults by increasing their options, but studies show these changes have had a negative impact on children. Divorce can damage parent-child relationships. Single parenthood and divorce often lead to economic instability and even poverty. Studies show that children from disrupted families are more susceptible to future emotional, economic, and educational problems. Of course not all children who come from single-parent households face these problems, and not all two-parent households are ideal. But more evidence is showing that the disintegration of the American family is producing undesired consequences for American children and society at large.

Finding solutions is not easy. Some propose that the government increase incentives for marrying; it could provide tax breaks for married couples and not penalize government-aid recipients who marry. Others support government-funded school programs that teach teenagers how to avoid pregnancy. Some urge the government to garnish fathers' wages or to create more economic opportunity for young men, particularly those in depressed urban areas, so they provide for the children they father. Both conservative and liberal Americans have suggested changing the cultural climate, turning back the clock to again socially condemn behavior that was once considered inappropriate.[19]

A favorite platform for American politicians in the 1990s has been "a return to family values." Although the government and other social institutions can help lessen the damaging effects of family disruption, Americans generally concede that they need to modify individual behavior and make different individual decisions to create more stable families.

Related information: questions 1, 3, 8

---

19. Ibid., 70–71.

3   • *Why does America experience so much juvenile delinquency*
     • *and so many gang problems? Don't parents control children?*
     • *Don't American children respect their parents?*

First, the point should be made that most American children and teen-agers respect their parents and are not involved in delinquent behavior.

Another important point is that physical discipline carries more of a stigma in America than it ever has. The difference between disciplining/ controlling and abusing children is a sensitive and debated topic in American society today. In general, today's parents rely less on corporal punishment than on talking and reasoning with their children. Some who come from cultures where physical discipline is considered normal, and even necessary, may therefore feel that American parents do not adequately control their children.

For those children who are delinquent, parents are often at least partially to blame. Some parents lack the know-how to discipline effectively. Unfortunately, too many are indifferent, negligent, or even abusive. Single parents or mothers and fathers in two-parent homes who work long hours—sometimes out of economic need—can find it difficult to monitor their children's activities and teach them mature behavior.

If children spend little time with parents, obviously other influences will command their attention. The media can and does influence children. Peers have always had an influence, but they tend to have even greater authority when parental presence is weak. Gangs, for example, serve as a kind of pseudo-family structure for some children who do not receive adequate guidance or support from home. Thus, parents can lose "control" of their children to outside people or circumstances.

However, parents are not wholly to blame for increased juvenile delinquency, which is also due in part to general societal trends. First, an emphasis on the importance of individual freedoms over collective authority has been growing in American society for several decades. Many teenagers today believe their activities—sexual, criminal, or otherwise—are their own business, not their parents'. With cynicism about government, law-enforcement, and other authority structures so prevalent, it is not surprising that some children scorn parental authority as well.

Also to blame are the related phenomena of poverty and educational, economic, and social discrimination. A disproportionate number of those involved in gang and other criminal activity are ethnic or poorer-class minorities: African and Hispanic Americans, South Pacific Islanders, etc. People who historically have been discriminated against may become involved in criminal activity because other means of making money seem unachievable or because they can find a form of acceptance in criminal associations. Inner cities, where interrelated forces of discrimination, poverty, and crime are most common, often breed criminal behavior. Violence in these areas can become a way of life for children who grow up carrying a gun for their own protection or for prestige.

Americans are trying to solve the many problems of juvenile delinquency. There is an increasing emphasis in American politics, cutting across the political spectrum, to "strengthen families"—within both the family unit and the greater community—as a response to juvenile delinquency. Numerous government-sponsored and private programs aimed at "at-risk" children attempt to give them guidance and support. Several programs offer friends and mentors to children from single-parent homes. In some states, parents who feel they cannot properly handle and discipline their children can also receive parental training. It is becoming obvious, as the juvenile justice system becomes overworked, that more preventative programs, community concern, and supervision for American children are necessary.

Related information: questions 2, 4

4 : *Why do you have such a problem with crime in America?*
  : *I'm afraid to travel there.*

Crime in America is admittedly a huge problem and is the primary social concern of many Americans today. However, America's crime problem should be put into perspective.

Crime has always been a major problem, but it is more reported now, partly because reporting systems are more sophisticated and partly because being a victim of crime—such as rape or domestic violence—carries less of a stigma than it did several decades ago. Many also perceive crime as being rampant in America because newscasts and other media focus heavily on the subject. Non-Americans see these reports and may get an inaccurate picture of the extent of crime in America.

According to recent reports, most Americans are as safe as they've ever been from violent crime.[20] Only certain segments of the population are committing and experiencing a great increase in violent crime. Recruited by gun-toting gangs and drug syndicates, young males (who are considered more prone to violence) have become responsible for *and* victimized by much of the violent crime in the last decades of the twentieth century. The fact that there are now more young men in the general population simply exacerbates the problem.

The "culture of poverty" so prevalent among some urban minority populations also contributes. A history of racial discrimination, the lack of quality education available, a perception that education is irrelevant, and a scarcity of jobs contribute to endemic poverty and social inequalities and often lead to backlash. Those in poverty, including more and more young males, sometimes turn to crime out of frustration, in an attempt to get their "fair share," or turn to drugs as an escape from reality. The fast money that results from selling drugs can be particularly appealing.

---

20. Aric Press, "A Crime as American as a Colt .45," *Newsweek* 124, no. 7 (15 August 1994): 23.

Increasing numbers of teenagers, in both urban and smaller communities, are joining gangs. Gang involvement is usually drug—and, therefore, money—related. But gangs also provide fellowship for youth who are not accepted elsewhere, hence the high proportion of minorities involved in gangs. Youth from disrupted families are also susceptible to gang recruitment. Most gang crimes are linked to drugs or territory disputes; members feel a need to protect with violence what little they have.

Overloaded law enforcement, court, and prison systems are limited in their effectiveness to capture, punish, and house criminals. The United States guarantees alleged criminals the right to a fair trial and due process of law, which contributes to delays and system overload. An overloaded system then leads to more plea bargaining, lighter sentencing, and early paroles for potential repeat offenders. In contrast, some countries have justice systems that measure out swifter punishment.

Many believe that violent television shows, movies, and video games contribute to the problem by modeling violent behavior. Simultaneously, the American media fiercely protects what it claims is its constitutional right to free speech. Others defend another constitutional right—the right to bear arms—but most homicides, particularly among teenage males, are committed with guns.[21] As violent crime increases, Americans will continue to debate what limits, if any, should be placed on these rights.

Americans are not apathetic to the crime problem, and many are attempting to find solutions. The technology, organization, and management of law enforcement and security have improved. Americans pressure politicians to make crime prevention and punishment a major priority. Congress has responded with stiffer laws and more funding for enforcement. Americans are also recognizing that, since crime is a soci-

---

21. According to a 1995 Justice Department report, *Juvenile Offenders and Victims: A National Report*, guns were used in 80 percent of homicides committed by American juveniles between 1984 and 1993. Report cited in Associated Press, "Kids Today Are Worse than Ever, Reno Says," (Brigham Young University) *Daily Universe*, 8 September 1995.

etal problem, it requires a society-wide solution. Neighbors are organizing neighborhood-watch programs and take-back-our-streets efforts, and numerous programs for "at-risk" kids are being developed and tested. In urban neighborhoods where community activities have dwindled, many teenagers get involved in crime because they "are bored." Some cities sponsor activities such as midnight basketball leagues in an attempt to keep kids out of trouble.

If you visit the United States—and there is no reason you shouldn't—you should be cautious, but you needn't be fearful. Literally millions of tourists visit popular areas such as Washington, D.C., which has a relatively high crime rate, without becoming victims of crime. In fact, almost all international tourists have enjoyable experiences and meet friendly people during their visits to the United States. Crime is not universal in intensity throughout the country. You can walk after dark in many places without fear of becoming a victim. However, in urban areas you should take precautions just as you would in areas of Mexico City, London, Moscow, or New Delhi.

Related information: questions 3, 5

5 : *Why do so many Americans own guns? Do Americans still have a "cowboy" mentality?*

The U.S. Constitution's Second Amendment guarantees American citizens the right to bear arms. Today more than eighty million Americans own guns,[22] and the National Rifle Association (NRA) is one of the most politically influential groups in the country. However, the fact remains that more than one-half of all homicides are committed with handguns. That translates into 12,000 American lives lost annually.[23]

---

22. Tom Morganthau, "Gun Control: Too Many Guns? or Too Few?" *Newsweek* 124, no. 7 (15 August 1994): 44.

23. U.S. Federal Bureau of Investigation statistic, cited in "Table No. 305. Mur-

Proposals to control gun access have raised a heated debate. Gun advocates, including NRA members, argue that criminals, not guns, kill. They claim the majority of owners use guns for sport or protection, not to commit crimes. Some even suggest that guns deter crime; for example, if there were a good chance that a home owner had a gun, a criminal would likely hesitate to break into that home. The desire to protect family and property with a firearm may constitute a "cowboy" mentality,[24] but as Americans feel more threatened by crime, some are adopting this way of thinking.

Conversely, other Americans feel guns should be more tightly regulated. They believe the Second Amendment applies to government-sponsored militias and the current interpretation of the amendment does not address today's social context. Although most Americans do not advocate abolishing guns, many believe closer government regulation would deter gun use and, thus, deter crime as well as accidental shootings.

Gun control is a sensitive issue because it involves interpreting a constitutional right. However, people are becoming more vocal about limiting gun purchases in some way. James Brady, Ronald Reagan's former press secretary who was shot in a presidential assassination attempt (1981), lobbied for passage of the Brady Handgun Violence Prevention Act, which established stricter regulations for purchasing handguns (1993). Other national laws have banned the sale of certain automatic and assault weapons. Gun advocates argue such laws are unconstitutional. Undoubtedly, as the threat of crime increases and the public calls for greater protection, the debate over guns will only become more heated.

Related information: question 4

---

der—Circumstances and Weapons Used or Cause of Death: 1980 to 1992," in *Statistical Abstract*, 201.

24. *"Cowboy" mentality* refers to the mindset of many early Americans when they settled America's frontier. Because few formal law-enforcement institutions were in place there, settlers often had to defend their property, their families, and themselves with firearms.

6 : *Describe your school system for us. Why don't U.S. schools focus more on fundamentals? on discipline?*

The U.S. school system includes the following stages:

- preschool (ages three or four)
- kindergarten (age five)
- elementary school (grades one through five/six, depending on the school)
- secondary school
  - junior high or middle school (grades six/seven through eight/nine)
  - high school (grades nine/ten through twelve)
- junior college or vocational training (two years), or
- college/university (at least four years).

Education is compulsory for ages five (kindergarten) through sixteen (about tenth grade). The majority of students complete their high school education at grade twelve (age seventeen or eighteen).

Although an aim of the U.S. government is to provide universal education, not all schools are equal. There are some national standards with which states must comply, but each state is responsible for its educational system and sets local standards. Even within a state, the implementation of these standards will vary according to region or school "district." Indeed, local districts and individual schools generally have considerable autonomy in determining how they structure their curricula to meet state-determined objectives. Therefore, there really is no single, uniform U.S. educational system. In U.S. schools you will find a wide range of curricula, facilities, teacher salaries, teacher qualifications, dropout rates, parental participation, student-to-teacher ratios, and funding.

Public schools are funded with tax dollars. Students may have to pay fees, but they are minimal. Private schools, including church-sponsored parochial schools, are funded by student tuition and private endowments. Because private schools generally spend more money per pupil, some Americans view private education as superior. However, good and bad schools exist in both categories—public and private.

Americans tend to view formal education as holistic. So in addition to emphasizing basic academic subjects, schools provide extracurricular activities: sports and recreation, music, drama, art, and others. Schools even teach such basic skills courses as driver's education, woodworking, and cooking. This broad focus of the U.S. educational system may make American schools seem less rigorous.

There have been a number of educational trends in the United States. Citizens concerned about a perceived lack of fundamentals have supported recurring back-to-basics movements. Perhaps the most famous was a public reaction to the Soviets launching Sputnik. Fearing the Soviets were winning the Cold War technology race, Americans pushed for more intensive math and science education.

The 1980s and 1990s have seen a trend toward greater cooperation between business and education and an emphasis on technology education. Many businesses have donated computers and other resources to schools. Educators are also heeding business leaders' advice when it comes to creating curricula. As a result, many teachers emphasize inquiry learning over content learning. Instead of encouraging rote memorization, teachers help students gain problem-solving skills and allow them to work cooperatively in groups. Many believe this training helps prepare students for the "real world," where they will have to search for information and cooperate with coworkers to solve problems. The fact that many students spend more time in cooperative activities and less time memorizing facts and figures may also make the U.S. system seem less rigorous.

Americans have always viewed schools as agents of "socialization," but the mission to socialize students has taken different forms. After schools were racially desegregated in the 1950s and 1960s, children who were mentally and physically challenged were also placed or "mainstreamed" into public schools. A more diverse student body has created demand for a more diverse curriculum. Some believe schools must develop curricula that give equal attention to the contributions of various social and ethnic groups, rather than simply concentrating on the contributions of Anglos. Others believe trying to include authors or historical figures from all backgrounds in an English or history class leaves little room for the "fundamentals" American students should know. Another debate sparked by America's diverse student body surrounds the issue of bilingual education—whether or not immigrant children attending public schools have the right to be taught in their native languages. Thus, educating America's diverse population has proven to be a difficult task.

Accelerated juvenile crime, teenage pregnancy, and the disintegration of traditional families, have led to a call for socialization in the form of "character education." With the perception that children are not receiving adequate training at home, there is an increasing demand for schools to teach morals, interpersonal skills, and self-discipline. But this demand comes at a difficult time.

Shrinking school budgets cannot pay for all desired social programs. Debates rage over which standards should be taught, particularly in regards to values, sex education, and individual "rights." While corporal punishment is accepted in some countries, most U.S. states now have laws against physical discipline in the classroom. Budget cuts have resulted in high student-to-teacher ratios in many schools. And children's interests are more fragmented than ever before. More after-school jobs and increased familial responsibilities in single-parent homes divert students' attention from schoolwork. Cable television, which offers hundreds of channels, and video games have the same effect. And students who deal with the emotional strain of neighborhood violence, family strife, and/or early sexual activity often have difficulty concentrating on what, in comparison, seems like trivial work.

The result is that schools and teachers are being stretched beyond their capacity. They cannot teach fundamentals and be parents and policemen. The majority of teachers and administrators are doing their best to meet the educational and disciplinary needs of their students, but Americans are beginning to realize that schools lack the resources to solve all of society's ills. As a result, a new back-to-basics movement is emerging. Many, including business leaders, are calling for schools to teach basic problem-solving, reading, and writing skills rather than focus on social programs.

Ironically, even with these increasing educational challenges, more Americans are going on to higher education than ever before. In 1960, only about 8 percent of Americans had completed four or more years of college, while in 1993, 22 percent had.[25] Although tuition at some institutions can be expensive, the U.S. college/university system is considered to be among the best and most accessible in the world. One unique aspect of U.S. higher education is its extensive system of junior colleges, two-year institutions that can serve as springboards to four-year colleges/universities and degrees. Critics of America's school system may abound, but it is preparing more students than ever before for higher academic achievement.

Related information: question 38

7 : *What are your courtship practices like? Your young people seem to have a great deal of freedom in their social relations.*

American youth courtship or "dating" practices vary from family to family. Parents usually determine when their child is old enough to date. Some parents allow children to date at a young age—in groups or with chaperones. Others prefer their children wait until about age sixteen. The average age to begin dating is probably between twelve and fifteen years.

The tradition has been for boys to ask girls for a date, but with greater emphasis on equality between the sexes, girls now feel freer to

---

25. U.S. Bureau of the Census, "Table No. 232. Educational Attainment, by Race and Ethnicity: 1960 to 1993," in *Statistical Abstract*, 157.

initiate dates. In the past, the boy normally came by the girl's home, met her parents, and told her parents where they were going and when they would be back. Although that practice continues, most youth today take a more casual approach, sometimes meeting at a designated place or calling for their dates without formally meeting the parents.

Most dates involve going to a movie or renting a home video, eating at a restaurant, going dancing, attending a concert, or going to a sporting or other event. Although drinking is technically illegal for Americans under age twenty-one, some American teenagers get together and consume alcohol. Sexual activity among dating teens is becoming more prevalent but is not universal.

Parents still may exercise their parental prerogative to disapprove of a boyfriend or girlfriend or counsel their child about dating. Many have strict rules about the time their children should be home at night, but by and large, American youth are given a great deal of freedom in choosing their dating partners and practices. And since many teens have part-time jobs, they enjoy a degree of independence in dating because they can fund their own activities.

American young adults, over the age of eighteen, have even more freedom in their dating. Many live away from their parents while working or going to college. Even if young adults still live at home, their parents typically respect their right to a relatively independent, private social life. Young adults often meet dating partners at college, in night-clubs, or at other social activities. When young adults decide to marry, they usually come to the decision as a couple and then announce that decision to their parents. Asking parental permission to marry is traditional but is becoming less common. More young adults are also choosing to live together rather than marry.

Another trend has emerged over the last four decades as the divorce rate in America has increased. More middle-aged adults are entering the "dating world," which in the past was predominated by teenagers and young adults.

Related information: question 8

8 : *We hear a lot about America's sexual promiscuity, high rate of sexually transmitted diseases (particularly AIDS), and large numbers of children born out of wedlock. Are these serious problems in your country?*

Movements advocating sexual freedom have recurred throughout American history and have usually come at times of great social upheaval. At the beginning of the twentieth century a sexual "revolution" was sparked by the shake-up of traditional values after the devastating World War I, the popularity of Sigmund Freud's theory that repression of sexual appetites can be harmful, and an increased emphasis on women's rights.

A similar revolution came about in the 1960s and 1970s: the controversial Vietnam War made many rethink their traditional values, the civil rights and women's movements preached individual freedoms, the Watergate scandal squelched Americans' faith in authority, and the Cold War's influence was still felt. The message of these tumultuous times was similar to that of the 1920s: "free love," "living for the moment," and sex as a form of "individual expression."

America's sexual revolution of the 1960s not only brought out in the open sexual activity that was already occurring; its messages promoted sexual activity outside of marriage. Now more Americans become sexually active and/or cohabit without the "need for a piece of paper" (a marriage certificate). Also due to the sexual revolution, the American media today is more open about sexually related topics; a series of court rulings in the 1960s allowed the media to portray more explicit material than before. Whether the proliferation of such materials reflects or fuels greater promiscuity—or both—is debated.

Indeed, the messages of the sexual revolution are still prevalent today. Statistics show these messages often drown out the message of religious institutions and other organizations that promote sexual abstinence outside of marriage: one study of students in grades 9–12 showed that

54 percent of all students (61 percent of males and 48 percent of fe-
males) had had sexual relations.[26]

America is reaping the consequences of promiscuous behavior. AIDS
and other sexually transmitted diseases with debilitating effects are spreading. Births to teenage mothers increased 27 percent between 1986 and
1991 alone.[27] And more tax dollars are being used to support single
mothers who cannot support themselves. Americans are becoming more
aware that "free love" carries major costs.

There are signs that behavior is changing in response to these problems. In 1992, births to girls ages 15–17 decreased slightly for the first
time in years, probably because of increased contraception use.[28] The
fear of contracting AIDS has led some Americans to change their sexual
behavior. AIDS has also led many schools to teach about "safe sex." Some
schools even distribute birth-control devices.

Schools' involvement in sex education has sparked controversy. The
argument over whose definition of "morality" should be taught in the
schools is a heated one among America's diverse population. Some argue
that teenagers will become sexually active no matter what, so distributing contraception is a natural function of the schools. Others claim that
the only "safe sex" is no sex and that abstinence should be taught in
schools as well.

It should be noted that a minority—but still substantial number—
of Americans maintain religious or personal convictions that sexual relations are to be reserved for marriage. In fact, an abstinence movement
has become more visible and vocal in America. Among supporters of the
movement are various religious organizations and "True Love Waits": an
organization that enlists tens of thousands of young people who pledge
to remain chaste. Some professional athletes, musicians, and actors have

---

26. Centers for Disease Control, "Sexual Behavior among High School Students—
United States, 1990," *Morbidity and Mortality Weekly Report* 40, nos. 51 and 52 (3 Janu-
ary 1992): 885–88.

27. Lewin, "Births to Young Teen-Agers."

28. National Center for Health Statistics, cited in Lewin, "Births to Young Teen-Agers."

come forward to support the movement. Decades after the "decadent 1920s," the moral pendulum swung back to more "traditional" sexual values. Perhaps the same will occur in the next few decades. This time, however, fear of undesired consequences, including AIDS and death, may be the primary force that moves the pendulum back.

Related information: questions 2, 7

9 : *How do you take care of your elderly? Why do you put them in homes for the aged?*

In the past, shorter life spans meant that the lives of American grandparents and grandchildren seldom overlapped for long. For people who lived longer, their children often served as caretakers. Now an overlap of three generations in American families is common, but generally speaking, Americans are experiencing greater independence between generations.

One reason for this change is increased mobility and urbanization. In their quest for jobs, children move from where they were raised, to distant cities or suburbs. This trend has lead to a greater focus on the immediate, nuclear family. Perhaps the greatest contributor to intergenerational independence is that people today live longer, healthier, more active lives. Americans now live to be an average of seventy-six years old and are shunning the idea that post-retirement years are their "twilight years." They want to be independent—to live their own lives and continue to contribute—and they do not want to be a "burden" to their children.

Most Americans plan and save early on to be financially independent after retirement. A longer career span (due to a higher mandatory retirement age) and retirement savings plans afford those who plan ahead varying degrees of financial independence. The creation of government programs to aid the elderly has also lessened dependence on kinship networks to provide financial support. The government taxes all working Americans to provide the elderly with "social security" in the form of post-retirement monthly income. The government also sponsors Medicare, which offers minimal subsidies to the elderly for health care. Thus, many children no longer plan to be their parents' only source of future financial support.

However, America's growing elderly population is stretching government funds. The number of elderly Americans is expected to triple by 2030 and will comprise 20 percent of the U.S. population.[29] The increasing political power of organizations such as the American Association of Retired Persons (AARP) likely will ensure that these programs continue in some form, but the government will find it increasingly difficult to subsidize care for the growing elderly population.

Certainly, there are those among America's elderly who are not independent—who have inadequate finances and/or need special care. Typically, American women live longer than their husbands, an average of almost seven years. Some cannot adequately care for themselves. Family members provide 80 percent of home care for America's elderly—male and female.[30] However, home care is not feasible for some elderly Americans who require special personal and medical attention. The costs in financial resources, emotional strain, and time, as well as the technology and medical knowledge required, can place a heavy burden on families. This is especially true in cases of advanced debilitating illness. Many families agonize over deciding what is best for an elderly parent or relative under such circumstances. They are torn between "caregiver burnout" and the guilt they feel for not personally providing daily care for loved ones.

Care centers or "homes," for the elderly are sometimes the best option. Retirement/nursing homes are a fast-growing service industry. Approximately 23,000 such homes exist in America with more than one million elderly residents.[31] The federal government pays some costs for

29. U.S. Bureau of the Census statistic, cited in Esther B. Fein, "Relatives Burning Out Caring for Aged at Home," *New York Times*, 19 December 1994, late edition, sec. B.

30. Fein, "Relatives Burning Out."

31. *The New Grolier Multimedia Encyclopedia*, CD-ROM release 6, s.v. "nursing home."

those residents who qualify for help because of inadequate income. Nursing homes are also federally regulated. Although not all care facilities are ideal, the best provide a clean, friendly atmosphere, competent medical care, and a variety of activities for their residents.

Again, how best to care for an elderly relative is not an easy decision. Many more individuals and societies will face similar decisions as improved health care and diet lead to longer life spans worldwide.

10 : *How can you have so many homeless, poor, and unemployed in a country that is so rich in resources?*

Presently in the United States, graphed income distribution looks like a bell. Most Americans fall somewhere in the middle class.[32] So by and large, America is a "wealthy" country.

But government officials and social scientists warn that America is becoming an increasingly two-tiered society. In the early 1990s, the number of Americans living in poverty was steadily increasing (to about 15 percent), the typical household income was falling, and the rich were getting richer while the poor were getting poorer. Perhaps the most disturbing aspect of these trends was that they took place during a period of overall economic growth. This increasing inequality is due to a number of factors.

For all our talk of equality, America's capitalist society simply does not reward individuals equally. The U.S. economic system is set up in such a way that if distribution of wealth were equal regardless of individuals' actions, efficiency and incentives for growth would be destroyed.

However, poverty cannot wholly be attributed to lack of individual effort. Increased international competition is blamed for loss of Ameri-

---

32. The following served as a general source for the information contained in this response: Jason DeParle, "Census Sees Falling Income and More Poor," *New York Times*, 7 October 1994, late edition, sec. A.

can jobs in certain industries. Some Americans are losing jobs to coun-
terparts overseas as U.S. companies downsize their workforce and/or
wages to compete more efficiently in the global market. Others receive
lower wages due to decreased unionization and the shift of U.S. jobs
from manufacturing to typically lower-paying service industries. And
though unemployment rates are not extremely high in America (about
6 to 7 percent), many Americans are "underemployed"; they are over-
qualified for their jobs and receive wages that are not consistent with
their experience and education.

A complex "culture of poverty" has also contributed to inequality.
It exists in areas where (1) people have not enjoyed a tradition of education or experienced equal opportunities for employment, (2) industries
have moved and left few job opportunities, (3) dependence on government welfare has undermined incentives to work, and (4) despair has
set in through generations. These and other factors affect people's
worldview to the point that they no longer believe they can succeed
economically.

Rural poverty has long been endemic in some areas of the United
States, particularly in the southeastern region. Inner-city areas, where
African Americans and other minority groups dominate, are also particularly susceptible to the culture of poverty. Single mothers of all races
have found themselves part of the poverty cycle in increasing numbers;
approximately 50 percent of America's single mothers live in poverty.[33]
American families with children are experiencing homelessness, poverty,
and unemployment to an extent not experienced since the Great Depression more than sixty years ago.

Limited help is available for the poor. To meet immediate needs,
public and private organizations have created shelters and soup kitchens. The U.S. government provides welfare assistance and is attempting
to increase training and other programs that encourage the poor to become financially independent as quickly as possible. Long-term solu-

---

33. Whitehead, "Quayle Was Right," 62.

tions have been slow in coming. The fact that certain poorer populations are increasingly turning to crime may force Americans to address seriously the problem of social inequalities.

Related information: question 34

11 : *Why is there such prejudice and hate between whites, blacks, and other ethnic groups in America?*

To be understood, prejudices between ethnic groups in America should be put in historical perspective.

For centuries, Caucasians—in many countries—felt their religions, intellect, sensitivities, and way of life were superior to those of other races; their laws reflected that feeling of superiority. Although the U.S. Declaration of Independence declared "all men are created equal," early U.S. laws allowed slavery, determined that slaves were equivalent to three-fifths of a white person in matters of taxation and representation, and limited the immigration of dark-skinned ethnic groups. Americans' legal and social treatment of Native Americans has similarly been characterized by ignorance, intolerance, and, yes, hatred. Even after the American Civil War, which resulted in a constitutional amendment abolishing slavery, legal and social discrimination persisted. The civil rights movement of the 1950s and 1960s helped bring an end to legal discrimination based on race (as well as on sex and religion) by prompting the passage of the Civil Rights Act (1964) and other legislation.

However, social and economic discrimination is not so easily abolished. Members of some minority groups are among America's poor in disproportionate numbers. This is due in part to limited educational and employment opportunities that have traditionally plagued them. Understandably, some American minorities resent "the white man" for their present predicament and have retaliated, sometimes through riots or demonstrations. Racial tensions between non-Caucasian ethnic groups are growing in some areas because groups compete for limited jobs and resources. Increased tensions between African-, Hispanic-, and Asian-American communities in southern California are just one example.

A famous American lyricist once wrote that people have to be "carefully taught" to hate and fear.[34] Indeed, racial discrimination is a learned behavior, usually passed from generation to generation. Those who have had little or limited personal contact with members of other races are particularly susceptible to thinking in negative stereotypes. Many only see obvious differences in skin color and mannerisms rather than our common humanity, interests, and concerns. However, it is probably an accurate statement that most Americans attempt to be less prejudiced about race and race relations than their ancestors. The U.S. press often focuses on white supremacists and other fringe or hate groups precisely because they are not typical.

A centuries-old legacy of hate and fear may be legally eradicated in one hundred years, but lingering individual prejudices could take generations to change. The passage of time may show that the legal and social are connected; even as discriminatory laws fostered prejudice, non-discriminatory laws may foster greater tolerance. Certainly racial desegregation has brought more Americans of different ethnic backgrounds into contact. Although universal tolerance may be an unrealistic goal, increased contact can bring increased knowledge, which may lead more Americans to judge others by "the content of their character" rather than by the color of their skin.[35]

Related information: questions 12, 66

34. Oscar Hammerstein II (lyricist) and Richard Rodgers (composer), "Carefully Taught," in *South Pacific* (New York: Williamson Music, Inc., 1956).

35. From Martin Luther King Jr.'s "I Have a Dream" speech delivered 28 August 1963 as the keynote address of the March on Washington, D.C., for Civil Rights, in *I Have a Dream: Writings and Speeches that Changed the World*, ed. James Melvin Washington (San Francisco: HarperSanFrancisco, 1992), 101–6.

12 $\vdots$ *Why are Indians among some of the poorest in your country?*

Many early settlers came to the United States to avoid oppression and poverty and to begin a new life, working land they could call their own. When they found native "Indians" had a claim to lands and resources, they often worked to undercut that claim out of greed, feelings of cultural superiority, and insecurity. Few rules or laws dictated fair interchange back then. Much of the interaction between Indians and early European settlers could be categorized as warfare, with injustices and atrocities committed by both groups. The Indian population began shrinking due to violent clashes, diseases introduced by the new settlers, and malnutrition brought on by a shrinking food supply.

White men, including the predominantly white U.S. government, largely dictated early treaties made with Indians. (The U.S. Senate ratified 370 treaties between 1778 and 1868.)[36] Even so, the U.S. government generally did not abide by the treaties it "negotiated" or imposed. In 1830, due to pressure from southern whites who wanted Indian land, the U.S. government forced eastern tribes to relocate in the western United States. More than 70,000 people were made to travel hundreds of miles and live on plots of what was considered unproductive land. Unaccustomed to a non-nomadic, agricultural lifestyle, many were thus forced to live an alien way of life. By the end of the nineteenth century, the majority of Indians were living on designated lands called "reservations."

For nearly one hundred years, the U.S. government cast itself in the role of caretaker. Its leaders adopted a paternalistic position, legislating "for the Indians' good," but much of that legislation was ineffective. Post-World War II policy was designed to decrease government services to Native Americans and assimilate them into the majority population.

---

36. Richard L. Worsnop, "Native Americans: Will the Columbus Quincentenary Highlight Their Problems?" *CQ Researcher* 2, no. 17 (8 May 1992): 393.

(Congress had declared Indians full U.S. citizens in 1924.) But the fact that Indians had been "put away," forced to live a foreign lifestyle, and basically forgotten by other Americans created unique needs. They experienced greater health problems, higher infant death rates, and lower life expectancies than the larger population, primarily because of inadequate income, housing, sanitation, nutrition, and medical care. The government made some attempts to develop low-cost housing and increase health-care availability on reservations. Nevertheless, most government programs did not take Indians' desires into account.

An "Indian power" movement began in the 1960s, about the time of the larger civil rights movement. Not all Indians (or *Native Americans*, as many now prefer to be called) were involved in the movement for autonomy, but most desired a greater voice in matters affecting them. In the 1970s, the U.S. government began a "self-determination" policy to increase the autonomy of tribal groups. Over the last twenty years or so, the government has increasingly recognized that Native Americans have the right and capacity to govern themselves. It has also given them more freedom to exploit or protect resources on tribal lands. Hundreds of nonprofit organizations now seek to protect the rights and serve the interests of Native Americans.[37]

Today the Native American population stands at approximately two million,[38] with about one-half living on 285 federal and state reservations around the United States.[39] Ironically, the lands allotted to tribes, which were once considered unproductive, have yielded rewards in the last several decades. Some tribes have successfully sued the U.S. government and won settlements for earlier land seizures. Some have developed industries on their lands, such as mining or oil, while casino gam-

37. *Minority Organizations: A National Directory,* 4th ed. (Garrett Park, Md.: Garrett Park Press, 1992).

38. U.S. Bureau of the Census, "Table 1. American Indian Population by Selected Tribes: 1990," in *1990 Census of Population: Characteristics of American Indians by Tribe and Language,* sect. 1, 1990 CP–3–7 (Wash., D.C.: Government Printing Office, 1994), 1.

39. *World Book Encyclopedia,* 1994 ed., s.v. "Indian, American."

bling has become a profitable industry on a few reservations. Tribes split profits from reservation industries (which are not taxed) among members or invest them in tribal funds that finance education and scholarships, create jobs, and improve health care. For the most part, reservations are now maintained not to keep Native Americans out of the larger society but to protect their land rights, limited sovereignty, and culture.

When discussing "Native American culture," one should remember that it is not homogenous; on the contrary, every tribe has very different traditions. Speaking in general terms, however, Native Americans have a unique worldview that emphasizes community and extended family, co-ownership of property, interdependence, and redistribution of wealth. In general, they are less individually oriented and driven to "get ahead" than other Americans. Some have found it difficult to reconcile traditional practices and values with the predominant culture outside of the reservation.

Complicating matters are mainstream institutions—some schools, for example—that have belittled and attempted to eradicate Native Americans' worldview, languages, religions, and traditions. Some U.S. educational and employment systems have yet to fully understand and tap the potential of Native Americans' unique strengths. On reservations, unemployment is still relatively high, as are school drop-out rates; some housing is substandard; and the rate of alcoholism is high. These are pervasive and serious problems yet to be solved, but they do not define Native American life.

To preserve their way of life, many have elected to stay on reservations, farming, raising livestock, running their own businesses, or working in reservation enterprises. In the western United States, some produce and sell native arts and crafts—paintings, hand-woven rugs, pottery, jewelry—to an increasing tourist market. Others work for mining, oil, or other industries located close to reservations. Some have left reservations for careers in business, higher education, law, or politics, at the local and national level. A portion of those who do not live on reservations maintain few ties to their traditional culture, but others work to increase Americans' awareness and support of Native American issues.

Native American issues have come in and gone out of style many times in American history, but a "renaissance" of sorts has been in progress in the latter decades of the twentieth century. The Native American population is growing, and the culture is resurging. The increasing popularity of the idea of cultural diversity has fostered pride in Native American history and culture as well. It appears U.S. government and society are learning that Native Americans are a people with admirable traditions and the right to be self-determining.

Related information: question 11

13 : *Why are Americans so "open" and extroverted—willing and anxious to talk about very personal things in public?*

Although some Americans are very private people, American society as a whole is probably worthy of the label "extroverted."

It may be helpful to remember that many early Americans immigrated to escape oppression in their home countries, including the oppression of free expression. Therefore, America's founding fathers included the right to free speech in the Constitution's First Amendment. Americans today are still fiercely protective of their right to say what they want, when and where they want. Certain laws and court rulings have placed limits on that right, but by and large Americans enjoy the legal right to be extremely "open."

In addition, Americans demand openness of others. Perhaps because of their ancestors' experiences in their homelands, they have long distrusted what they perceive to be "closed" institutions. More recent controversies (including President Richard Nixon's Watergate scandal, the Vietnam War, and Central Intelligence Agency scandals) have fueled Americans' distrust and have increased the demand for forthrightness from public institutions and figures. America relies largely on its free press, relatively unfettered by government regulation, to keep politicians and government accountable. The press has also found it profitable to delve into the *personal* lives of public figures—and not just those of politicians. Tabloids, magazines, and television shows that discuss the private lives of entertainers have grown in popularity. Right or wrong, Americans have come to believe that a thorough examination of one's life is the price one pays for living in the public eye.

In addition, the acceptance of psychology and psychotherapy as legitimate scientific fields has heavily influenced twentieth-century America. Many Americans now believe that airing emotional problems is healthy and that suppressing feelings and thoughts can be harmful.

In the 1990s, the popularity of radio and television talk shows, on which "everyday" people discuss personal problems, attests to the need some Americans feel to rid themselves of emotional "baggage." Many seem to believe confronting their problems publicly not only helps them but may also help others dealing with similar problems. And Americans tune in by the millions, some to participate in a kind of vicarious therapeutic experience and others to engage in what has been termed "verbal voyeurism."

Related information: question 14

14 : *Why do Americans rely so much on psychotherapy and drugs? Why is there such a market for illegal drugs? I'm aware that my country supplies yours with drugs, but we wouldn't if the United States didn't provide such a large market.*

Speaking very generally, Americans before the 1960s lived in more stable families and neighborhoods, but the close-knit communities and families that once offered a stable support system have vanished for many Americans. Americans have become more mobile, often moving to urban areas and experiencing greater anonymity in their neighborhoods.

Divorce has similarly disrupted community and family support networks. Removed from extended family and close friends, many Americans still deal with the problems of modern life in the "old-fashioned" way: with the help of personal fortitude and/or religious beliefs and institutions.

Yet a rapidly changing American society has led some to question traditional support systems, including family, community, and church. A number of Americans today look to counselors or psychologists for support in dealing with the stresses of modern life: unsatisfactory personal relationships, unemployment, economic problems, etc. People who visited psychologists were once labeled "crazy," but Americans' interest in psychotherapy has increased steadily in the latter half of the twentieth century. Today, seeking counseling is somewhat commonplace. The popularity of television talk shows in the 1990s, on which psychologists and counselors offer advice about relationships, self-improvement, and more, illustrates Americans' increasing interest in finding outside help for their problems.

Others turn to prescription drugs for help. Over the last few decades, scientists have become increasingly aware of the link between brain chemistry and such common psychological disorders as depression. A huge industry now produces prescription medications that help to restore a more normal chemical balance in the brain. Hundreds of thousands of Americans, who were previously prone to depression and other disorders, now swear by the effectiveness of drugs such as Prozac and lithium. Taking prescription drugs to normalize moods and behavior—ideally done in conjunction with professional therapy—no longer carries the stigma it once did.

Again, it should be emphasized that most Americans deal with stress and problems in normal and healthy ways. Nevertheless, some Americans seek affiliation and deal with their stress in deviant ways, through gang or other criminal activity. Many try to escape their problems through illicit or prescription drug abuse or alcohol abuse. Although drug abuse existed long before the 1960s, the "counterculture" movement of the 1960s and 1970s popularized the practice. The movement emphasized instant gratification and promoted drug use as a harmless—even healthy—way to escape the troubled world. Today many Americans continue to abuse drugs for various reasons. They seek affiliation with a certain crowd, want to escape emotional problems, enjoy the "high" accompanying drug use, or feel immune to or are unaware of potential harmful effects.

Reliance on illegal drugs constitutes a serious problem in the United States, as it does elsewhere. America provides a highly profitable market for drug producers, syndicates, and dealers; exporting drugs to America is a major industry for some countries. Many rightly blame U.S. drug demand and money for fueling the drug trade. However, the drug problem needs to be addressed from all sides: supply and demand, domestic and international.

The U.S. government, believing that accessibility increases demand, maintains a law against underage drinking and the distribution, sale, and use of illicit drugs. The government also seeks the cooperation of government and law enforcement officials in other countries to decrease the supply flowing into the United States. Concurrently, America has taken advantage of the post-Cold War climate to employ civil, military, and intelligence resources in the "drug war." Americans have also worked to decrease demand through public education and media campaigns; many campaigns attempt to influence children before they can become involved in drug use. And private and government moneys fund drug rehabilitation and counseling programs.

Americans are making an effort, but the extent of the drug problem worldwide attests to the fact that curtailing drug distribution and use is a highly interdependent effort, requiring the efforts of all nations and peoples involved.

Related information: questions 13, 19

15 : *Do American television shows and movies accurately portray American life? Why do you export your media? Many people in my country feel the U.S. media corrupts our youth; plus it gives Americans a bad image.*

The answer to the first question is yes and no. American media both reflects and distorts American lifestyles and values.

Americans like to see themselves portrayed in the media. Whether it is a therapeutic or voyeuristic experience is difficult to say, but Americans want to see people handling timely problems in a realistic way. Thus, movies and television shows often treat current social problems such as race relations, divorce, rape, drug abuse, murder, infidelity, physical and sexual abuse, and other current social problems. A television trend in the 1990s is the reenacting of real-life emergency or crime situations. Another popular trend has been television and radio talk shows, on which people discuss and try to find answers to personal problems. Because most American media is in the private sector, it is largely financed through advertising. "Crisis TV" tends to draw audiences, which in turn draws advertising dollars, but the media portrays problems so often that non-U.S. residents may mistakenly think Americans live their lives in a constant state of crisis.

In addition to watching real-life dramas, Americans enjoy escapism. They enjoy watching people wealthier and better looking than they are, who deal with improbable situations. "Fantasy" shows allow many to escape their problems and concerns for a while. Much of what is exported to other countries falls into the fantasy category, which may also create a distorted picture of America. Obviously, not all Americans live in huge mansions, wear beautiful clothes, and plot to ruin their family members, like the characters on *Dallas* and *Dynasty*. Similarly, not all Americans live on the beach and look wonderful in a swimming suit, like the people on *Baywatch*.

Much of the media exported from America tends to create inaccurate stereotypes of Americans and may contain messages many consider immoral. But Americans will continue to make movies and television shows of lesser quality because (1) Americans are guaranteed by their constitution the right to free speech, and American filmmakers are constantly fighting what they perceive to be government "censorship"; and (2) they can make money. Lesser quality shows will also continue to be exported; there is a market overseas and money to be made. In some ways—because the demand for it exists—the media pollution crossing national borders is harder to control than environmental pollution.

Actually, part of the justification for American information and cultural programs, such as U.S. Information Agency, Fulbright, teacher-exchange, and other programs, is to counteract the stereotypes and negative effects of exported material that portrays Americans in an inaccurate light.

The bad is usually what receives the greatest attention, but to be fair, the American media has exported quality programs as well. People who could never go to a large city to see a musical or play, symphony, opera, or ballet, can see such productions in their homes, and American educational programs have helped teach millions of children worldwide. With the increasing technology available for personal use—the computer Internet system, compact discs, VCRs, CD-ROMs, etc.—Americans will export their media to an even greater extent, but be assured that along with the bad will surely come some good.

Related information: chapter 1 introduction

16 : *Why are Americans obsessed with health and fitness? Why are they so worried about their appearance?*

Ironically, people often consider Americans "obsessed" with health and fitness, but generally speaking, Americans are more overweight and less fit than ever before. Studies show that in some health-related areas, such as abstaining from smoking and regulating public smoking, Americans are far ahead of their international neighbors. However, studies also show that the majority of Americans do not purposefully diet or exercise.

Experts attribute a lack of fitness to several factors, chief among them being Americans' sedentary lifestyle. Many Americans spend their days at the office behind a desk and their evenings at home in front of a television. Even between work and home they are sitting on a subway, on a bus, or in a car. In their desire to save time and money, Americans also tend to eat cheap "fast food" or prepackaged, convenient meals; unfortunately, the cheapest, fastest food is often the least healthy.

However, many Americans do exercise and diet, and many do so to improve their appearance. Media images of thin female and muscular male models and actors have set a high standard of beauty and are at least partly to blame for U.S. society's undue emphasis on outward appearance. Some Americans, in an attempt to be one of the "beautiful people," become obsessed with appearance, and thus with diet and exercise, to an unhealthy extent. The fact that eating disorders such as anorexia nervosa and bulimia are somewhat commonplace illustrates that Americans can become obsessed with appearance.

But many Americans who exercise and eat healthily do so primarily to feel better. Those who live sedentary lives often feel a need to be more active. Others regard exercise as a kind of insurance policy, as more studies show that exercise reduces the risk of health problems such as heart attack and breast cancer. Some simply enjoy the camaraderie and friendly competition of sports. Most Americans who exercise on a regular basis are motivated by a combination of all of these objectives; they want to look and feel better, be healthier, and have fun.

Americans' interest in health has fueled a number of exercise and diet trends over the last few decades: jogging, aerobics, crash diets, diet pills, mega-doses of vitamins, fiber, calcium, sugar substitutes, nonfat foods, etc. But Americans are learning, often the hard way, that being obsessed with any one aspect of diet or exercise can be unhealthy and that moderation in what they eat and do is the key to good health.

17 : *Why are American sports so violent?*

Of the major U.S. sports, football is probably the only one that could be termed "violent." Baseball players incite an occasional bench-clearing brawl and basketball players may elbow an opponent in the jaw. Boxing and hockey are violent but are just as popular, if not more so, outside the United States. Other sports that are growing in popularity in the United States—figure skating, golf, and tennis—are largely nonviolent. Presumably, then, this question chiefly concerns American-style football.

Football began in the 1820s as a game played between university students every fall—a kind of rugby mixed with soccer, with few rules and little equipment.[40] Football today is highly regulated, and pads and equipment are used to protect players from injury, but it is still, admittedly, a violent game. Some Americans dislike it for that fact. However, football remains the number-one spectator sport in America.

Some believe the violence of football reflects capitalist America's "obsession" with fierce competition and aggression. Others believe watching football is a cathartic experience for Americans; they can release their pent-up frustrations vicariously by watching football players tackle and pound each other on the field. Some theorize that football is a metaphor for America's beginnings: the taming of the frontier. Men fight the elements and opposing forces to move across an expanse of land and claim some as their own. The names of some professional teams reflect this metaphor: Raiders, Chargers, Cowboys, Forty-Niners, etc. So is the popular game of football violent because Americans are capitalists? because they need a release from daily pressures? because they are reenacting the violent frontier days of our country? Maybe.

Few fans stop to analyze the "whys" behind football. Though they admit it is violent, most believe "it's only a game." They claim to enjoy watching football because it involves strategy, skill, and physical prowess. They also enjoy associating with a team and other fans; being a foot-

---

40. Richard G. Powers, "Sports and American Culture," in *Making America*, 281–83.

ball fan is way to vicariously "belong." If Americans watch football primarily to see men tackle, pound, and hit each other or to work out their capitalist aggression, few are willing to admit it.

18 : *Don't you live in a very materialistic, "throw-away" society?*

If asked to make a list of priorities, most Americans would place their personal relationships first, but Americans also look forward to and enjoy having material things: nice clothing, well-furnished homes, appliances, video and audio equipment, cars and recreational vehicles, and other luxuries. Sometimes they allow their desire for "things" to affect their choices and priorities. To the extent that their desire for material possessions overrides their other priorities, Americans are deserving of the label "materialistic."

Americans' desire to accumulate material goods largely stems from a love of convenience. They want things that make their lives more comfortable, easier. Many of those conveniences are things they can easily discard: fast-food cartons and other disposable packaging, disposable razors, disposable diapers, even disposable contact lenses. So yes, America is a throw-away society.

However, educational and public awareness campaigns, as well as news reports, have helped Americans realize that the things they dispose of don't "disappear" but have a definite environmental impact. Americans are also becoming increasingly aware that the world's resources are not endless. More Americans are concerned about leaving their children a resource-rich, clean world to live in. So recycling efforts are increasing. State governments encourage citizens to use more energy-efficient public transportation or to carpool. Businesses are rethinking and redesigning packaging and product formulas. Many businesses have made "environmentally safe," "recyclable," or "made from recycled materials" a major selling point of their products.

However, some Americans aren't participating in recycling and other efforts because doing so isn't convenient. Collectively, Americans certainly do not deserve to be called "frugal," but many are making small strides toward more economical use of resources.

Related information: questions 51, 70

19 : *Americans seem to be better "doers" than "thinkers." On the whole, they seem more pragmatic than spiritual and philosophical. Is this an accurate assessment?*

America's "roots" tell something about American society today. Early U.S. settlers included an elite class, constituted of educated businessmen and landowners. Some of America's great thinkers were among this class, including its "founding fathers," who developed a philosophically sound, democratic constitution. However, the majority of U.S. settlers were not intellectuals, nor were they from the bourgeoisie or aristocracy. They were from the peasant class or religious minority groups or, in the case of African Americans, were brought over as slaves. These people were not professed thinkers; they were doers, working hard for survival, greater opportunity, and material security, generation after generation. This work has generally led to a better standard of living as well as more opportunities for education.

To a certain extent, American life is still directed toward the goal of attaining material security and greater opportunities. So yes, Americans are pragmatic. For example, in higher education Americans often "specialize" in preparation for a career. Conversely, Europeans and others spend more time gaining a general education, studying history, philosophy, art, and culture. The more broadly educated European may believe Americans are not philosophic or idea oriented. That generalization may be true.

However, speaking in terms of dichotomies—thinking versus doing, pragmatic versus philosophical and spiritual—may be a bit simplistic.

In American life, these activities and qualities are inextricably linked. American minds first conceived of and then produced many of the world's great inventions. U.S. universities, "think tanks," and research facilities are world-renowned and have made important contributions to the world's population, through practical research and thought applied to problem solving. Authors such as Walt Whitman, Ralph Waldo Emerson, Emily Dickinson, William Faulkner, John Steinbeck, and Toni Morrison have made great contributions to the world of thought through literature. The relatively large number of Nobel prizes won by Americans in all areas—physics, chemistry, physiology/medicine, economics, literature, and peace—is another testament to the value placed on the applied thought of Americans.

With regards to spirituality, religiosity is not extensively portrayed in American media, but many Americans consider themselves very religious, spiritual people. Nearly 70 percent of American adults are members of a church or synagogue.[41] But again, religion is another area where the spiritual and the pragmatic overlap for Americans. For example, the "Protestant ethic" of hard work, self-discipline, self-sacrifice, and thrift was religiously motivated but reaped very practical rewards for early Americans. While many would argue that the Protestant ethic is diminishing, many would agree that religious ideals in America still bisect the secular and practical. One example is the impact today of various religious groups involved in community development and action projects. U.S. religious denominations also sponsor more missionaries throughout the world than do sects in any other country. Much of the missionary work performed includes not only proselytization but humanitarian service in the form of health-care, literacy, and other development projects.

It is true that Americans, on the whole, have struggled somewhat to strike a balance between the pragmatic and the philosophical or spiri-

41. Princeton Religion Research Center statistic, cited in U.S. Bureau of the Census, "Table No. 85. Religious Preference, Church Membership, and Attendance: 1957 to 1991," in *Statistical Abstract*, 70.

tual. During the 1960s and 1970s, a youth-oriented, counterculture movement decried the "establishment" and American materialism. Most participants found, however, that they could not meet their physical needs devoting so much time and effort to the contemplative or spiritual. The 1980s were considered a very materialistic time in American history; in fact, some of those who participated in "getting gain" were the very people who led the counterculture movement a decade earlier. The late 1980s and 1990s have witnessed something of a yearning for the spiritual again. One poll showed that more than three-fourths of Americans believe the United States is "in a moral and spiritual decline."[42] The "New Age" movement and the political "Religious Right" have appealed to some Americans in their search for spirituality.

Is the assessment accurate that Americans are pragmatic rather than philosophical and spiritual? Generally speaking, probably so, but speaking in dichotomies fails to highlight the lives and contributions of millions of Americans who value a combination of these qualities and activities—both the spiritual and the practical, both thinking and doing.

Related information: question 14

20 : *Why aren't more Americans interested in and informed about what happens outside your country's borders? Even your news focuses mainly on national events.*

Many Americans are more concerned about happenings in their local communities than in the world at large. They are aware of other countries only as highlighted in the media during a crisis, and if something does not directly influence American life or interests, they generally do not take the time to learn about it. They also fail to keep current on

---

42. *Newsweek* poll results, cited in Howard Fineman, "The Virtuecrats," *Newsweek* 123, no. 24 (13 June 1994): 31.

what is happening in different parts of the United States. While this is regrettable, it means Americans try to understand the part of the world that most directly affects them and that they can directly influence. The same could be said for most of the world's populace.

Those Americans who are interested in world events have voiced frustration that major U.S. magazines, newspapers, and television newscasts do not contain substantive international news. Although Americans may have to search, they can find more in-depth, global media coverage. *The New York Times*, Cable News Network (CNN), and public television's *The MacNeil–Lehrer NewsHour* are just a few sources. Certainly the spread of cable television, computer news services, and international linkages through the infobahn/information superhighway are helping "shrink" the globe. These information sources will likely serve to increase Americans' global awareness.

But in their rush to deal with daily immediate concerns, many Americans do not take the opportunity to seek out these sources; they turn instead to quick news coverage on television or in local newspapers, which contain limited international coverage. Most Americans get the bulk of their current-events information from brief television or radio newscasts.

America's isolationist tendencies may partially be due to its geographic location. Americans have only two immediate neighbors, Canada and Mexico (about which most Americans know admittedly very little), and are separated from most other countries by the world's largest oceans. In the past, being isolated geographically meant being isolated informationally, and perhaps Americans have simply carried on that tradition.

However, their apathy can largely be attributed to the fact that the United States impacts many other countries economically, socially, politically, and culturally, because of its power and outreach, while it is not reciprocally influenced by individual countries' actions to the same extent. An event in the Philippines may have little or no exposure in the American press unless it is a crisis or of broad interest. Conversely, many Filipinos know relatively more about the United States, through their press, because certain U.S. actions or policies have affected their country. This phenomenon may account for, and even help fuel, the ethnocentric attitude of some Americans that "they need to learn about us, but we don't necessarily need to learn about them."

Unfortunately, due to all of these factors—fast-paced lifestyles requiring convenient information, the preeminence of local concerns, America's relative power and geographic position, and ethnocentric attitudes—the majority of Americans are underinformed about the rest of the world.

Related information: chapter 1 introduction

21 : *Why don't Americans learn our language and more about our culture while they are here? Why don't people from the United States living in our country socialize or mix with our people?*

Some Americans fail to learn about a language or culture, or to socialize with native residents, out of ethnocentrism. Because many are proud of the "American way" and think it is the best or *only* way, they may not learn about or adopt other cultures' practices. Ethnocentrism leads to an interesting paradox. When foreigners come to the United States, many Americans feel they should "jump into the melting pot" by learning English and adopting American ways. However, when Americans go to another country, they generally do not believe the reverse applies to them. Obviously, ethnocentrism and prejudice are linked; often the same people who do not befriend individuals from different ethnic groups in the United States show no interest in a different culture, language, or people when visiting or living abroad.

However, there are other, perhaps less offensive, reasons for Americans' seeming lack of interest in other cultures.

Because English is the *lingua franca, de facto,* of business and diplomacy, some Americans see no need to learn another language. In Pakistan, for example, many Pakistanis learn English in school and speak English better than American business representatives could ever speak Urdu. And organizations often will not invest in an employee's learning a language when that language is not necessary to doing business in a country. Some Americans are simply too self-conscious to speak an unfamiliar language; they do not want to appear stupid. What they fail to understand is that they appear more ignorant by not making an effort to learn.

Americans working abroad also work in a "foreign" environment, with different pressures and problems than those to which they are accustomed. After a day's work, they want to relax and feel "at home." Without intending to be exclusive or isolationist, they may unwind by surrounding themselves with the familiar—people who speak English, understand their ways, and enjoy the same food.

In Washington, D.C., where international employees abound, one witnesses the same tendency. After 6:00 P.M., employees of embassies, multinational corporations, the World Bank, and other organizations retreat with fellow countrymen to "national islands." They congregate in familiar places, speak their native language, eat familiar food, and socialize with familiar people to relax. All over the United States ethnic groups from Asia, Latin America, and Europe have settled in neighborhoods or enclaves where they can preserve their traditional language and culture. Americans similarly tend to congregate when they are abroad.

Americans abroad may seem aloof because some companies entice American employees away from friends, family, and familiarity with incentives for working overseas. Incentives may include a relatively high salary and amenities such as homes, cars, or maids that average citizens cannot afford. In cities where the risk of crime or terrorism is great, employers often safeguard their employees by housing them in isolated and expensive areas where security is tight.

U.S. government and businesses also send many Americans abroad to work specifically with business, academic, and/or governmental leaders. Working with the "elite" class tends to isolate these Americans from citizens who are not in a position of power.

With all of this said, however, Americans would learn more about a country if they would learn the language and socialize with native residents. Those who don't, pass up some wonderful educational and social opportunities. Currently, increased international competition is forcing more American representatives to learn the languages of their overseas contacts and be more culturally adept. And advocates of foreign-language study have apparently had an impact on the U.S. educational system: high-school-student participation in foreign-language study has grown substantially over the last few decades and appears to be on the rise, due in part to stricter university/college entrance requirements.[43] Perhaps Americans are learning some valuable lessons from past failures of international security, development, and trade activities.

22 : *Whom do Americans most admire? Who are their heroes?*

In some countries, the people most admired are those born into notoriety or wealth—royalty, for example. Americans differ in their tendency to admire the "self-made" man or woman. An admiration for ambition springs, at least partially, from America's beginnings. Most American immigrants came with relatively little material wealth in hopes of making a better life for their families. Those who obtained the "American dream" of increased wealth or influence were regarded as having exceptional talent, intellect, and drive. Perhaps this admiration also springs from our democratic system; if all men and women are created equal, then those who rise above must be exceptional and worthy of esteem. So American heroes have tended to be those who succeed in transferring talent, physical prowess, or leadership into fame, wealth, or power.

A respected American author and historian has said, "Celebrities are people who make news, but heroes are people who make

---

43. Jean Seligmann, "Speaking in Tongues," *Newsweek Special Edition: Education: A Consumer's Handbook* 116, no. 28 (fall/winter 1990): 36.

history."[44] However, many Americans—young Americans particularly—tend to regard celebrities as heroes. Athletes, movie and television stars, and musicians often top their lists. Many also regard as heroes those politicians who led the United States through unusually trying times: George Washington, Abraham Lincoln, Franklin Delano Roosevelt, and John F. Kennedy. Although Americans admire the accomplishments of great thinkers, such as writers and scientists, intellectuals have not captured Americans' attention to the extent that others have, perhaps because the American press has not appointed them "celebrities"—because their accomplishments are not accompanied by pageantry and publicity.

Under the watchful eye of an increasingly vigilant press, some traditional American celebrity-heroes have fallen from grace. Admired businessmen have been arrested for unlawful dealings. Revered sports figures have been jailed for serious crimes. Movie stars, in general, are notorious for unstable personal lives. Rock musicians have committed suicide and died of drug overdoses. Americans are increasingly cynical about politicians after the Vietnam War, the Nixon administration's Watergate scandal, the Reagan administration's Iran-Contra scandal, and widespread charges of political and personal corruption. Even public figures with relatively "clean" backgrounds undergo the scrutiny of the press and do not always emerge spotless. As traditional celebrity-heroes have failed to live up to their image, the majority of Americans are becoming increasingly cynical about the worthiness of any individual to serve as a role model and hero.

However, even as the media has uncovered some of the more sordid activities of American "heroes," the international media has also exposed Americans to new heroes: leaders of independence or civil rights movements abroad, athletes who overcome hardships to excel in the Olympic Games, astronauts and cosmonauts, and more.

---

44. Daniel Boorstin quoted in Ponchitta Pierce, "Who Are Our Heroes?" *Parade Magazine*, 6 August 1995, 4.

Some traditional celebrity-heroes are disclaiming their status as heroes or role models. Several years ago, a professional basketball player created controversy when he told his young fans that he did not want to be their role model. Many Americans believed he had an obligation to serve as an example because of his high public profile. But he had a point. Perhaps instead of looking to celebrities as heroes and role models, Americans will look more to those people with whom they interact everyday—parents, teachers, siblings, coworkers, and friends—or to those who make history rather than headlines.

CHAPTER TWO

TWO

AMERICAN GOVERNMENT

Explaining to non-Americans the nature of the U.S. system of government—its policies, its actions, and even its decisions not to act in certain matters—is no easy task. American political tradition, culture, and processes provide a unique context for government action and policy. They determine how issues are raised, who takes what position on the issues, and how policy differences are ultimately resolved.

Most non-Americans are familiar with some aspects of the U.S. political system. Do not assume, however, that familiarity with political institutions or leading political figures indicates a comprehensive understanding of the political system. American institutions are significantly different from the political institutions of most other countries. Therefore, do not hesitate to explain some very basic facts—American elections, terms of office, or the nature of constituencies, for example—even to individuals who seem reasonably well informed about American government. Indeed, most non-Americans do not understand the full complexity of the workings of the U.S. government: the interrelationships between the three independent branches of government, as well as the interrelationships between the national and state governments; the differences in point of view stemming from the different constituencies that elect congressional representatives, senators, and the president; the impact of the American system of elections; and the role of political parties in our system. In many cases, explaining some basic facts can help clarify an issue.

An important element of our system of government, which may strike many non-Americans as unusual, is the reverence and stature we give the U.S. Constitution. Some foreign countries, including the United Kingdom, do not have a written constitution. The British system of government is based on unwritten tradition and acts of Parliament (laws), which establish fundamental rights and relationships. Most countries—nondemocratic and democratic—have constitutions, but these documents generally have not acquired the legal and cultural status that the United States's has.

The U.S. Constitution is the world's oldest functioning written constitution and, because of its longevity, Americans have developed a certain reverence for the document. The Constitution is a broad outline of how the U.S. government functions. It specifies the rights of individuals and state governments, but it does not provide detailed statements of policies. Because the process for amending the Constitution is difficult, Americans have not altered it much throughout the two centuries of its existence. In many countries, altering the constitution requires only a vote of the parliament, and because most other constitutions are comparatively more detailed, written constitutional changes are more frequent. Also, the less democratic a country, the more easily—and in many cases the more frequently—the fundamental charter can be and is changed. As a result, citizens of other nations generally do not revere their constitutions to the same extent that Americans do.

Although Americans have great respect for the Constitution, they have altered it in ways other than the formal and cumbersome process of amendment. Congress and the president, through the legislative process, constantly give new meaning to the Constitution. Furthermore, the courts, and particularly the Supreme Court, constantly and concretely interpret its provisions as specific issues are adjudicated. Overall, however, the government follows a strong tradition of operating within the fundamental parameters defined by this document.

The relationship between levels of government is another important aspect of the U.S. political system that is often difficult for non-Americans to understand. While some countries have attempted to duplicate America's federal system (Germany after 1945, for example), few non-Americans understand the importance and complexity of the federal-state relationship. In most other countries, provinces or "states" (in American terminology) are simply administrative units of the national government. Even when local officials are elected, their powers and authorities are determined and regulated by the central government.

In the United States, state governments are recognized as sovereign entities that have rights and powers independent of the federal government. This difference reflects both U.S. political history (the existence of thirteen original colonies, each jealous of their individual rights and privileges, coming together to form a unified federal country) and the desire of the country's founding fathers to balance and separate governmental powers in order to prevent the rise of tyranny in any form. As a result, state governments have absolute powers in certain areas; marriage and family law, education, and adjudication and punishment of most criminal acts are solely the prerogative of state governments. In some areas, however, the federal government has sole power, e.g., controlling currency, protecting national security, and conducting foreign policy. In some areas, federal and state governments share powers. For example, construction and maintenance of major highways is funded principally through federal tax revenues, and the federal government sets national highway standards, but determination of routes and supervision of construction and maintenance is primarily a state-government function.

Many of the questions asked by non-Americans may well involve understanding the relationship between state and federal governments. For example, American laws and practice regarding the death penalty for certain crimes (question 33) is only understandable with an appreciation of the federal-state relationship. While the Supreme Court has set standards regarding the imposition of capital punishment, almost all death-penalty cases involve crimes that are a violation of state, not federal, laws. Furthermore, the administration of legal executions is principally a state function.

Presently, the attitudes of U.S. citizens toward government in general and toward the federal government in particular have created a period of turmoil and change for the American political system. In recent years, Americans have developed a deep cynicism about our elected political leaders and a profound distrust of government.

One need only look at how government officials are depicted in American films in the 1990s to see how pervasive that cynicism has become. The thesis of Oliver Stone's film *JFK* (1991) is that faceless government bureaucrats, probably in collusion with pro-Castro Cubans, conducted a massive, evil conspiracy in masterminding and carrying out the assassination of John F. Kennedy. In *The Pelican Brief* (1994), conspirators within the White House attempt to alter government policies through illegal means, illicit political contributions, and a cover-up involving murder. *Dave* (1993) involves efforts to conceal the president's incapacitation by finding a look-alike to appear in public, in place of the president, so that his aides can continue running the country. *The Distinguished Gentleman* (1992) is the account of a congressman, elected through a series of comic accidents, who uncovers corruption and malfeasance in the halls of Congress. In the movie *Quiz Show* (1994), senators appear as background to the main drama, but they are depicted as timid, unprincipled, and detached. In *Clear and Present Danger* (1994), White House officials are involved in secret and illegal agreements with leaders of Latin American drug cartels, and as a result, the lives of innocent American soldiers and government officials are lost.

Even considering the "creative license" that filmmakers exercise to bend, color, and—in some cases—invent "facts" to make an interesting story, these films would not have a broad appeal if they did not reflect at least some measure of what is perceived as reality. Keep in mind in answering questions of non-Americans that many of them have seen these and similar motion pictures, and their perceptions of the U.S. system of government will be influenced by that exposure.

Americans' cynicism and distrust is reflected in the fact that some 49 percent of Americans think the Central Intelligence Agency (CIA) was somehow involved in the assassination of President John F. Kennedy (1963). More than one-half of all Americans believe flying saucers are real, and a good portion of these people think the government is covering up proof of their existence. A respected White House correspondent said on a national radio show that death squads were operating within the Justice Department and that she knew a man who was killed by federal thugs. A high-powered team of attorneys defending former football star O. J. Simpson (who was tried and acquitted in 1995 for allegedly committing two murders) built the entire defense case on the claim that their client was the victim of a sinister police plot to frame him with fabricated evidence.[1]

This distrust of and cynicism about U.S. government officials is the result of a number of factors. First, conspiracies involving prominent leaders have been highly publicized, e.g., the Watergate scandal (1972–74), which resulted in the resignation of Richard Nixon as president, and the Iran-Contra scandal (1986), which involved CIA and White House officials in illegal actions. These cases give credence to conspiracy theories. It is a reflection of the strength of our democracy that such scandals were discovered (with considerable difficulty) and made public and that officials involved were punished or forced to leave office. Although such incidents are infrequent and involve few individuals, they have served to undermine trust in elected and appointed officials.

A second element contributing to Americans' disaffection with their political leaders is the growing complexity of government and the widening separation between Americans and their elected representatives. For most Americans, the principal exposure to their political leaders is through thirty-second sound and video bites on television. Even con-

---

1. The information in this paragraph is taken from Liz Spayd, "Welcome to the State of Paranoia: Why America Wallows in Waco and Whitewater," *Washington Post*, Sunday, 23 July 1995, sec. C.

gressional representatives are increasingly remote from their constituents. The number of members of the House of Representatives has remained constant at 435 since the 1910 census, but the population of a single congressional district has increased from about 37,000 in 1790, to 211,000 in 1910, to more than 570,000 constituents per representative in 1990.[2] Furthermore, members of Congress are required to spend considerable time in Washington, D.C., dealing with legislation, and this limits their direct contact with constituents.

A third factor in this growing disaffection with the political process is the gridlock in Washington between Congress and the president and within Congress. American political parties have traditionally been largely nonideological—in contrast to those in most other democratic countries. For the most part, the two American political parties are broad-based, inclusive coalitions whose primary unifying purpose is to win elections and thus gain control of the executive or legislative branch of government. Party loyalty is not particularly strong, and most individuals identify only loosely with one or the other party. There are few "card-carrying" members of either party. To win the majority and receive a mandate to govern in such a two-party system, both parties are pushed toward the political center. The larger the constituency of an elective office, the stronger is the pressure to move toward the center. With a national constituency, presidential candidates must hold the center to win. Likewise, members of the Senate generally tend to be more moderate than members of the House of Representatives.

One of the most serious problems nationally has been the weakening of the political middle. In the past, there were always extremists on

2. U.S. Bureau of the Census statistic, cited in U.S. Congress, House of Representatives, Committee on House Administration, "Table 4–1. Size of the House of Representatives and Representation Ratio, 1789–1990," in *History of the United States House of Representatives, 1789–1994*, 103d Cong., 2d sess., 1994, H. Doc. 103–324, 63. Following the admission of Alaska and Hawaii to the Union in 1959, the House was temporarily enlarged. However, the size reverted back to 435 seats following the 1960 census; see page 61 n. 26.

the left and right of the political spectrum, but a strong and solid "center" succeeded in producing the compromises necessary to any democratic system. Over the past decade, the ideological extremes have grown and the center has declined. Some of this political polarization reflects changes in the attitudes and values of Americans. Some is the result of partisan manipulation to gain political advantage in elections. Some of this polarization represents the growth of single-issue politics. For example, many in the pro-choice and pro-life factions of the abortion debate consider a candidate's stand on abortion as the sole reason to vote for or against that candidate. Similarly, some members of the pro-gun lobby vote for or against a candidate based on the candidate's stand on gun-control legislation. The relatively recent proliferation of talk-radio programs that feed on and foster extremism has also contributed to political polarization. Indeed, all of these factors have contributed to the growing difficulty in reaching compromise on key issues, both in Congress and between Congress and the president.

A fourth element that has contributed to growing cynicism regarding our elected officials is the connection between money and politics. The cost of conducting a presidential campaign in the age of television has reached astronomical proportions. Even senatorial and congressional campaigns cost several million dollars. Although in the aftermath of the Watergate scandal Americans instituted a system for public financing of presidential campaigns, those funds provide only a small portion of what is necessary to carry out political activities. As a result, elected political officials must spend inordinate amounts of time raising funds for campaigns. This requires appealing to individuals and political-action committees that are linked with special interests. Despite efforts to draw a line between campaigning and governing, under the present system there can be no separation.

Because of the importance of special interests in financing political campaigns, these interests and the individuals who represent them in Washington (lobbyists) have considerable influence over legislation and policy in Washington and in the fifty state capitals. They have access to the political leaders in both the legislative and the executive branches of government. Furthermore, their resources give them the ability to influence public opinion through print and electronic media advertisements and to mobilize "grassroots" campaigns for or against particular policies and legislation. The massive media campaign of the health-insurance industry against health-care reform in 1993 and 1994 is just one of the many examples that can be cited.

The strength of American democracy is that it provides the framework within which political, economic, and social issues can be debated and resolved. Americans' cynicism about the federal government is leading to a reconsideration of the role Washington should play—of which governmental tasks are best handled by the federal government and which should be handled by state and local governments. This reconsideration may well lead to the revitalization of our state governments. The levels of government closest to the people may be best able to deal with their needs. The debate and reconsideration that is taking place in the United States is similar to the major reevaluation taking place in the European Union. The sixteen countries there are debating "devolution": which governing functions should be left to national governments and which should be handled by the central European Union administration in Brussels.

Non-Americans from developed, established democracies will see that the U.S. and their own systems of government are dealing with similar problems and difficulties. How Americans are responding to these concerns is of great interest to these individuals. For non-Americans from nondemocratic countries, the strength, vibrancy, and complexity of America's democratic system is both difficult to understand and wondrous to behold. With all of the weaknesses and difficulties our political system now faces, it is still a vibrant political system.

23 : *With such diversity in your population, how can you have only a two-party political system?*

The U.S. party system likely seems strange, particularly because countries with less cultural diversity have dozens of political parties competing for members—Italy and Central and South American countries, for example. Some attribute the dominance of two parties to the United States's reliance on a single-member-district/plurality-vote system. Under this system, geographical areas are split into constituencies. Only one legislative candidate is elected from each constituency by a simple majority/plurality of votes. Other nations have a proportional representation system. Political parties are granted legislature seats in proportion to the votes they receive in a general election. One party may receive a majority of the votes and the majority of the seats, but seats are allocated to most other parties receiving votes as well. This system tends to produce representation for a number of parties. The U.S. system results in a heavy preference for majority—Democratic and Republican—party candidates.

There is some question, however, as to whether the principal cause of the perpetuation of the two-party system is the single-member/plurality vote or Americans' general satisfaction with the system. The two-party system provides Americans with fairly stable political leadership. In addition, Americans—for all of their cultural diversity—have a relatively unified political vision, which focuses primarily on promoting democracy and economic prosperity. And even if Americans do not necessarily agree with every aspect of a party's "platform" or leadership, they seem generally satisfied with the present system of working out ideological differences. Like England, which has essentially a two-party system, and Mexico, which only now is breaking from an essentially one-party system, America works out its power struggles and ideological wars within—rather than between—parties. Indeed, the Democratic and Republican parties have long served as umbrella organizations, containing members who hold a range of views, from liberal to conservative, and providing a flexible framework for internal compromise.

Historically, Republicans have been considered more conservative, favoring less government control and regulation and more private enterprise. In the past, the commercial class and middle- and upper-class Americans have been the primary supporters of the Republican party. Democrats have been considered more liberal and have historically favored collective solutions to social problems and public-sector development. Lower- and middle-class Americans, labor unions, and minorities have been strong supporters of the Democratic party. However, in terms of demographics, strict characterizations of party members today are less predictable. Many minorities (Cuban Americans, for example) now support the Republican party and the more successful labor unions (Teamsters, for example) have turned quite conservative. Today, both parties are more pragmatic. They both concede that government intervention is necessary to an extent, but neither party is willing to call for large increases in government involvement or spending.

However, during the 1980s and 1990s, there was a growing trend within the Republican party to move toward greater conservative ideological unity. The congressional elections of 1994 gave Republicans control of the House of Representatives for the first time in forty-two years and control of the Senate for the first time in eight years. The program pursued by the congressional Republicans following the elections reflected a greater degree of ideological focus and party cohesion than the American political scene had witnessed for some time. At the same time, within the Republican party, Christian conservatives and other groups with a strong conservative ideological agenda gained greater influence. A few conservative Democrats joined the Republican party, expressing the view that the Republican party more closely represented their ideological views. Whether these trends will continue and the Republican party will become an ideologically based party in the European tradition, however, remains to be seen. The Democratic party, for the most part, continues to remain a very broadly inclusive political grouping.

The description of the Democratic party by American humorist Will Rogers still appears to be largely true: "I am not a member of any organized party—I am a Democrat."[3]

Although some Americans are fervent members of one party or the other, party membership is not permanent. To be recognized as a member of a political party and to be eligible to vote, Americans simply register with their local government at neighborhood registration posts. Most register as either Republicans, Democrats, or—if they feel no particular party loyalty—Independents. More and more local governments are distributing to voters computer-generated identification cards that list their party affiliation. However, Americans who want to switch parties can; membership is loose and informal.

In preliminary (or primary) elections, voters in most American states can only vote for candidates from their party, but in a final election they can vote for candidates from different parties. The 1988 presidential election showed that voters cross party lines in major elections: although 48 percent of Americans identified themselves as Democrats and only 41 percent identified themselves as Republicans, Republican presidential candidate George Bush won 53 percent of the popular vote.[4]

Even politicians switch sides. Elected officials depend on their constituents to remain in office, not necessarily on their party. Therefore, they may vote differently on an issue than the majority of their party members, if their constituents request such a move. It is not uncommon to see Republicans and Democrats form coalitions in Congress to fight against other Democratic/Republican coalitions in order to pass a law.

---

3. Suzy Platt, ed., *Repectfully Quoted: A Dictionary of Quotations Requested from the Congressional Research Service* (Wash., D.C.: Library of Congress, 1989), 85.

4. Elections Research Center statistic, cited in U.S. Bureau of the Census, "Table No. 423. Vote Cast for President, by Major Political Party: 1936 to 1992," in *Statistical Abstract of the United States 1994*, 114th ed. (Wash., D.C.: Government Printing Office, 1994), 269; Center for Political Studies, University of Michigan at Ann Arbor statistic, cited in U.S. Bureau of the Census, "Table No. 446. Political Party Identification of the Adult Population, by Degree of Attachment, 1970 to 1992, and by Selected Characteristics, 1992," in *Statistical Abstract*, 286

Americans can support other political parties besides the dominant two. Some register as members of the communist, socialist, libertarian, and other parties, but these parties do not enjoy the widespread organization or the financial backing that the major parties do, and again, the winner-take-all voting system tends to work against them. Candidates from these parties generally have not succeeded in developing a wide power base or in winning national elections, even though their candidacies occasionally have altered electoral outcomes.

There is some evidence that, when they feel Republican and Democratic candidates are "not listening" or do not represent their interests, Americans have supported third-party candidates. In 1968, American Independent presidential candidate George Wallace gained almost 14 percent of the popular vote; in 1980, Independent presidential candidate John Anderson received almost 7 percent; and in 1992, Texas billionaire and Independent presidential candidate Ross Perot gained nearly 19 percent.[5] Building on his 1992 showing, Perot formed a third party (1995), the Independence party, in preparation for the 1996 presidential campaign.

Since the end of the Cold War, Americans have turned their attention to domestic problems, and they generally are not happy with how the national government is managing those problems. As an anti-Washington, D.C., sentiment grows among Americans it will be interesting to see if third-party candidates, promising a political change, continue to gain support.

Related information: chapter 2 introduction

---

5. Elections Research Center statistic, cited in *Time Almanac*, 1994 CD-ROM reference ed., s.v. "Vote Cast for President, by Political Parties: 1920–1992."

24 :
How do people become president in your country? Some of your past presidents appear to have had little practical political experience: Carter was a peanut farmer, Reagan was an actor, and Clinton didn't serve in the U.S. military.

U.S. presidents over the last few decades have come from a variety of backgrounds, but most have had extensive political and leadership experience.

Jimmy Carter was a peanut farmer, but he was also a U.S. Navy officer and a nuclear engineer. In addition, he had been active in local and state politics for years, serving as a Georgia state senator and as governor of Georgia before his election as president.

Ronald Reagan served as president of the U.S. actors' union—the Screen Actors Guild—and as governor of California for two terms. He also worked to rebuild the Republican party after Nixon's Watergate scandal and develop the political support necessary to win the Republican presidential nomination in 1980 and 1984.

George Bush was an honored naval pilot during World War II and had a long political career in both elected and appointed offices. He served as a U.S. congressman, director of the Central Intelligence Agency, permanent U.S. representative to the United Nations, and U.S. envoy to China. He also spent two terms as vice president under Reagan before being elected president in 1988.

Bill Clinton did not serve in the military during the Vietnam War, but he graduated from the prestigious Yale Law School, was a Rhodes scholar, served on the campaign staffs of two presidential nominees, served as Arkansas attorney general, and was elected governor of that state at age thirty-two.

To be elected, all of these men, and other past presidents, had to (1) demonstrate party loyalty, (2) solicit party support and contributions, (3) communicate their message effectively to the general public and special-interest groups, and (4) organize a knowledgeable campaign team to work on local, state, and national levels. By constructing a successful campaign, they gained enough support to win their parties' primary elections and, eventually, the national election.

Although a presidential candidate's experience is important, the media is becoming more and more influential in presidential campaigns. Perhaps the greatest indication of the media's increasing influence came in 1960, when a debate between John F. Kennedy and a more experienced politician, Richard Nixon, was broadcast. The fact that Nixon looked unshaven and haggard compared to the young and tan Kennedy swayed public opinion. Since then, a great deal of power has passed to campaign communication specialists or "handlers," who work to present a positive image of their candidate to the public. They feed the media "sound bites" that communicate their candidate's message powerfully and memorably.

It is possible for a relative newcomer to win a national political race. Carter emphasized that he was a Washington "outsider" in 1976 after the Watergate scandal made Americans distrustful of Washington politicians. In fact, as Americans become more cynical about Washington "insiders," being a newcomer has become somewhat of an advantage, but even outsiders must have the resources to build a strong campaign organization. Billionaire Ross Perot, who ran as an Independent, was the surprise presidential candidate of 1992. His personal financial resources and reputation as a successful businessman helped him build a nationwide network of support. Even though he did not win the election, he won enough support (almost 19 percent of the popular vote)[6] to change the dynamics of the race. And he showed that a candidate's having political experience is not necessary or even desirable in the minds of some voters.

---

6. Ibid.

25 : *If yours is a participatory form of government, why don't
     more people vote in elections? In our country it's a law to
     register and vote.*

Low voter turnout is a real problem in the United States.[7] The percentage of voting-age Americans who voted in presidential elections fell from almost 63 percent in 1960 to 50 percent in 1988. The 1992 percentage was 55 percent—the largest voting percentage since 1972.[8] However, that recent high is still relatively low.

Speculation abounds about why Americans fail to vote, but studies show that the main reason is indifference on the part of U.S. citizens. For the most part, Americans do not have strong feelings about *not* voting. They simply feel distanced from politics. They believe the government is not responsive to ordinary citizens, and thus, they are apathetic. What many do not seem to realize is that not voting can have as much influence as voting; by not voting, citizens affect an election but not in the way they might choose.

Some think voter turnout would increase if eligible voters felt more connected to politics and less like outsiders. They claim the media could involve voters in the election process by providing them with substantive information—focusing on issues that affect voters and not on candidates' personalities or scandal. In addition, some believe the current U.S. voter registration system is too inconvenient and could be made more accessible. Currently, prospective voters have to register, usually at neighborhood registration posts, before they can vote. Some measures have been taken to make the process more convenient. In 1993, Congress passed the "Motor-Voter" Registration Act, which requires states

---

7. The following served as a general source for the information contained in this response: Ruy A. Teixeira, "Voter Turnout in America: Ten Myths," *Brookings Review* 10, no. 4 (fall 1992): 28–31.

8. U.S. Bureau of the Census, "Table No. 449. Participation in Elections for President and U.S. Representatives: 1932 to 1992," in *Statistical Abstract*, 288.

to provide voter-registration services at driver's license bureaus; thus, drivers can apply for a license and register to vote at the same location. Some argue that even more Americans would vote if mail-in registration procedures were more readily available as well.

It is less likely that U.S. lawmakers will pass a law requiring Americans to vote. The majority of Americans regard voting, and refraining from voting, as a right and would protest any attempt to force them into the voting booth.

26 : *How does your government function?*

One of the main concerns of America's "founding fathers"—the authors of the U.S. Constitution—was preventing despotism. As they outlined a government structure, they did not want to provide opportunities for a single government authority to become tyrannical. Therefore, they distributed power between government at the state and national (federal) levels and between branches of government at the federal level.

The Constitution gives the federal government broad powers: to defend the nation, regulate commerce, control currency, impose taxes, and more. The fifty states also have governing powers excepting those specifically withheld from them or delegated to the federal government. The federal government has three branches—legislative, executive, and judicial—that are roughly mirrored by branches of government at the state level. Ideally these branches are meant to "check and balance" each other.

Two groups form the federal legislative branch, or Congress. The House of Representatives contains 435 members representing all fifty states; the number of representatives elected from each state depends on that state's proportion of the national population and is adjusted every ten years. The Senate contains one hundred members, two from each state. The duties of Congress are varied. Congress makes national law and investigates how laws are carried out; confirms the president's appointment of individuals to certain positions, such as ambassador posts and the Supreme Court; approves treaties made by the president with foreign governments; and controls the budget by approving government spending and taxing. In addition to serving national interests, congressional representatives are supposed to serve the interests of voters from their areas.

The executive branch is led by the chief executive—the president. The president appoints, with the advice and consent of the Senate, department or "cabinet" leaders, agency leaders, ambassadors, and Supreme Court justices. He also serves as commander in chief of the U.S. armed forces and, therefore, is ultimately responsible for national security. He has the major responsibility of carrying out foreign policy, interacting with world leaders, and supervising treaty negotiations, although treaties and many policies must be approved by Congress. In addition to recommending the legislative agenda in Congress, the president can veto laws passed by Congress, but Congress can overturn that veto with a two-thirds vote in the Senate and the House.

The Supreme Court is the judicial branch of the federal government. The Court is made up of nine justices appointed for life by the president and approved by the Senate. It adjudicates legal cases that were heard in lower courts and appealed. In effect, it makes policy through its decisions and interprets ambiguous constitutional law. In addition, the Court exercises the power to declare laws passed by Congress and state legislatures "unconstitutional."

Although the branches of government are supposed to "check and balance" each other, at times some branches have exercised more power than others. The amount of power exercised by a given branch depends on the social circumstances, people in power, and public sentiment during a given time. For example, during the 1950s and 1960s, under the leadership of a strong chief justice, the Supreme Court exercised considerable influence in the area of civil rights. During times of crisis and societal upheaval, presidents have exercised greater power than at other times: Abraham Lincoln during the Civil War; Theodore Roosevelt and

Woodrow Wilson during the early 1900s; Franklin Delano Roosevelt during World War II; and Richard Nixon during the Vietnam War. Near the end of the Watergate scandal and the unpopular Vietnam War, Congress and the American public began to believe that immediate past presidents had exercised too much unchecked power, and Congress took back some "control," most notably by passing the War Powers Resolution (1973), which limited the president's ability to send U.S. troops abroad. (The constitutionality of that act has never been challenged before the Supreme Court, but many doubt it would survive such a challenge.) In the 1990s, state governments called for greater autonomy and a decrease in federal authority.

Thus, the balance of power between government branches and between state and federal government fluctuates. Certainly, the U.S. government does not function perfectly or equally well at all times, and the three-branch system tends to slow government action. That slowness can be frustrating, but the authors of the U.S. Constitution meant for government to work slowly and deliberately—better that way, they felt, than to work rashly and tyrannically.

Related information: questions 23, 59; chapter 2 introduction

27 : Is the American government responsive to the needs of the people?

The answer to this question is both yes and no. Congressional representatives and the president rely on voter satisfaction to remain in office. So elected officials must be responsive to their constituents, or they could lose their jobs.

However, politicians tend to hear and respond to organized Americans more than individual Americans. The concerns of business and other special-interest groups, known as "lobbies," often receive priority over those of individuals. The influence of special-interest groups has been stronger during some periods of history than during others. For example, at the turn of the twentieth century many Americans felt as if they were victims of big business. They also saw political parties as corrupt and self-serving and, therefore, organized into special-interest groups to initiate social reforms and fight corruption. These groups promoted causes such as workers' rights (particularly for women and children), women's suffrage, temperance, consumers' rights, conservation, and business regulation.

A somewhat similar movement happened after Watergate and the Vietnam War. People saw the government as corrupt and unresponsive and organized into special-interest groups to initiate social reform. From 1961 to 1987, the number of lobbyists representing business or special-interest groups grew from 365 to 23,011.[9] This increase also came about, in part, because participants in different civil rights movements began organizing to gain political influence.

Laws limit the political maneuverings of these groups but still leave room for well-organized groups to influence politicians by promising votes or donating campaign funds or other favors. Even so, in the end a politician's constituents may have the final say. For example, the National Rifle Association has always been a powerful lobby in Washington, D.C., but with the increase in gun-related crime, more Americans are supporting laws to control gun purchases. In the past, the tobacco lobby has been one of the most powerful business lobbies; it fights anti-smoking legislation and cuts in government subsidies to tobacco farmers. But as the health risks of tobacco use become more apparent, Americans are calling for less preferential treatment for the industry and increased government regulation of smoking is following.

Another way Americans can organize to influence legislation is through initiative and referendum. Through the *initiative* process, the people can write a petition proposing a law; if a designated percentage of

---

9. Joseph Hogan, "The 'No-Win Presidency' and Contemporary Presidential-Congressional Relationships," in *Explaining American Politics: Issues and Interpretations*, ed. Robert Williams (London and New York: Routledge, 1990), 46.

citizens sign the petition, the proposed law is put to a vote. Through the *referendum* process, the people can directly vote for or against the proposed law. The *initiative and referendum* process is, of course, the process in which both of these steps are combined—the people directly introduce a law and vote on it. Lawmaking through initiative and referendum is not an option nationwide, but many states and cities allow it, though procedures may vary. For instance, in some states, a proposed law that has passed through the initiative phase must be approved by the state legislature before being put to a public vote. In some areas, lawmakers are required to use the referendum procedure when proposing certain types of legislation, i.e., amendments to the state constitution, tax proposals, and bond issues. Although initiative and referendum is a rather expensive way to legislate, in terms of time and other resources spent, it is a way the people can "work around" government if they feel the government is not responsive.

28 : *If America is one of richest nations, why can't it balance its budget?*

In the last decades of the twentieth century, as the U.S. deficit has risen to huge proportions, U.S. citizens have increasingly demanded that the government balance the budget. But demanding a balanced budget and actually balancing the budget are two different things.

Politicians have introduced numerous plans to balance the budget. Some have even proposed a constitutional amendment that would require Congress to work within the limits of a balanced budget. But most plans postpone spending cuts or increased taxes for several years. Such delays give special-interest groups and politicians time to change the plans and/or allow the government to keep spending until the law goes into effect. For example, the constitutional amendment to balance the budget proposed in 1995 would not have required a balanced budget until 2002.

Government-funded benefits that drain the budget go not only to the poor but to Americans in the middle and even the upper classes. Few Americans are willing to give up their share of what they feel to be "entitlements." And because politicians depend on the public for their jobs, they do not want to anger voters by eliminating or reducing programs that benefit voters. Politicians also fear raising taxes, which would anger voters but would be necessary to balance the budget.

Neither do politicians want to risk offending powerful special-interest groups such as the American Association of Retired Persons (AARP), which supports health-care subsidies for the elderly. As the number of special-interest groups has grown, so have their demands on the budget.

In addition, plans by each political party to cut the deficit and balance the budget have met with opposition from the rival party. In this divisive issue involving taxing and funding for public programs, politicians tend to take sides.

There is enough blame to go around. At fault are Americans who want a balanced budget but do not want taxes raised or programs cut, as well as politicians who are afraid to offend voters and who place their reelection before the nation's future.

Related information: question 27

29 : *How can you have good security for diplomacy and intelligence with your Freedom of Information Act and government officials and journalists who reveal government secrets?*

The American people know that certain information must be kept out of the public realm for security reasons, but the dilemma of any democratic society is that citizens believe they also have a right to be informed of government activities. Many are suspicious of closed negotiations and distrust government officials to reveal the entire truth about their dealings. Given the past record of government officials—stretching back to the time when the United States were British colonies—Americans have some basis for their distrust. But achieving a balance between the information disclosed publicly and the information classified for intelligence and diplomacy reasons is difficult.

During the latter half of the twentieth century, several "sunshine laws" were passed to open government records and meetings to the public. The Freedom of Information Act (1966) is just one of those laws. It requires government agencies to make information in their files available to citizens asking for it. However, the law does not allow the release of information that would put national security at risk or violate an individual's right to privacy. (The U.S. Congress has passed several privacy acts to protect private information about citizens from being made public.) Since the act was passed into law, journalists, businesspeople, and other citizens have placed numerous demands on government offices to service requests for information. Unfortunately, confusion about the classification of information has led to the unauthorized dispersal of some information. However, since the act was passed, the information-access system has been refined and will likely continue to be refined.

Government officials have also deliberately leaked information related to diplomacy and intelligence operations. Some of these leaks are the result of regrettable indiscretions or, more seriously, malice. But officials also leak information to measure public reaction to a proposed policy or agreement before they approve or reject it. In political circles, such leaks are considered more practical than unethical.

As to the media's role in information leakage, the U.S. media sees itself as a "watchdog" that keeps the government from overstepping its bounds. This relationship often leads to clashes between the media and government as the media argues for the public's right to know and the government claims the right to guard information that it considers to be sensitive. Clashes have intensified in the information era when information can be broadcast worldwide simultaneously. During the Persian Gulf War (1990–91), the U.S. government tried to restrict journalists' access to information and photo opportunities, citing security considerations.

They knew Saddam Hussein could watch news coverage via the Cable News Network (CNN) just as easily as U.S. citizens could. However, journalists felt government censorship tactics during the war were excessive.

The majority of Americans who are information "gatekeepers" in America—government officials and journalists—try to strike a balance. They want to keep the American public informed of policy decisions and actions while not jeopardizing security and diplomatic interests. The ideal is that all of the factors involved—probing journalists, vigilant government officials, and information laws—will balance each other in the end and provide U.S. citizens with just enough information. They don't always achieve the ideal, but Americans are still trying.

30 : *Is your CIA really necessary in the post-Cold War environment?*

In an increasingly interdependent world, information gathered through intelligence is vital for almost all countries. Although the superpower duel is over, the regional tensions that have developed since the end of the Cold War illustrate that having accurate intelligence to inform decision making is still necessary. For the most part, governments cannot depend on the media and other "open" sources to provide reliable information; in addition, nonintelligence sources cannot always gain access to sensitive areas that intelligence agents have been able to tap.

While most Americans would agree that intelligence is necessary, many are calling for an end to the Central Intelligence Agency (CIA) or, at least, for a significant cutback of its funding and activities.

As previously classified documents from the Cold War are being declassified, there are indications that the CIA was not as effective in gathering information about the Soviets as was previously thought. Therefore, people are questioning if the amount of resources invested in the agency is warranted.

Additionally, many see the CIA as a "renegade" agency and an "old boys' network" that holds itself above the law. Americans generally distrust any secretive organization, and the CIA has been increasingly criticized. The 1994 Ames spy scandal particularly damaged its reputation. It was estimated that Aldrich Ames, a former CIA officer, sold secrets to the Soviets concerning dozens of intelligence operations and the identities of Soviets who were reporting to the CIA, at least ten of whom were killed. But when the agency conducted a self-review after the scandal was publicized, the agency's director blamed the scandal on a system breakdown rather than on individuals. CIA officials received relatively lenient reprimands. This lack of accountability shocked Americans and led to demands for the reform and even the end of the agency. Those demands increased when, in 1995, it was made public that (1) the CIA continued to fund the Guatemalan army's intelligence agency after the president had officially suspended such aid and (2) a Guatemalan colonel on the CIA payroll was involved in the deaths of an American expatriate and an antigovernment guerrilla married to an American.

The government spends only about 10 percent of its *intelligence* budget on the CIA.[10] Twelve other military and civilian agencies or bureaus make up the rest of the intelligence community. Some have suggested that the CIA be disbanded and its functions distributed among the other agencies. Others argue that, as long as there are states with the intention and the potential to damage U.S. interests, the CIA is the best-equipped agency to seek out denied information about those states. Even so, most agree that if the CIA is to continue, a drastic change in its operations is needed: both the agency and its employees must be more accountable to the government and the public for their actions.

---

10. Editorial, "The C.I.A. Club Needs a Cleanup," *New York Times*, 30 September 1994.

31 :
Is it true that millions of your own people can't afford medical care? Why don't you have a government health-care program? You say you are against socialism, but in this case, socialized medicine would seem more humane.

Americans spend a high amount on health care, per capita, compared to citizens of other countries. High costs are due to inflation and the increasing sophistication of medicine in terms of technology, equipment, and personnel skills. Although the United States claims to offer the best medical care in the world, it is the only major industrialized country that does not offer some form of national health care or insurance. For the majority of working Americans, most of their medical expenses are covered through health insurance paid for by themselves and their employers. But many who are not employed or whose employers do not offer insurance are unable to afford rising health-care costs. The number of uninsured Americans is estimated at approximately forty million.[11]

Since 1966, two government programs that offer health insurance to the elderly and the poor who meet certain qualifications have been in place: Medicare and Medicaid. Both programs are funded by taxes but have proven to be more costly than was originally planned. For example, in 1965 it was estimated that Medicare hospital insurance would cost the government $9 billion in 1990; the actual cost was $67 billion.[12]

---

11. U.S. Bureau of the Census statistic for 1993, cited in Janice Sommerville, "Census: Almost 40 Million Uninsured Americans," *American Medical News* 37, no. 41 (7 November 1994): 13. Some critics, however, contend that this number does not accurately portray the number of *chronically* uninsured Americans, which could be as low as 3 percent of the nation's population (nine million people); see, for example, Irwin M. Stelzer, "What Health-Care Crisis?" *Commentary* 97, no. 2 (February 1994): 19–24. Still others believe census bureau statistics underestimate the number of uninsured Americans, particularly children. The Employees Benefit Research Institute places estimates of the uninsured at 16 percent of the nation's population (forty-one million people); see *Facts on File* 55, no. 2827 (2 February 1995): page 67 col. A2.

12. Peter G. Peterson, "Remember Cost Control," *Newsweek* 124, no. 4 (25 July 1994): 21.

The number of Americans benefiting from government subsidies is so large that politicians find it difficult to cut spending without people protesting. However, many feel the current system pays benefits to some who are not truly needy and leaves out the working poor who make too much money to qualify for Medicaid but not enough to pay for their own insurance.

Many agree that some kind of nationwide health-care reform is necessary. Some believe health insurance should be guaranteed and universal—that it is part of Americans' constitutional right to life, liberty, and the pursuit of happiness. Some say universally extending health care is a humanitarian issue. Others believe it is a matter of keeping the nation strong and viable as a world power. Many point to the Canadian system as an example of an effective government-run system.

Other Americans believe insurance coverage is a privilege, not a right. Many think health-care reform would limit their choices concerning the doctors they can see and decrease the quality of care they receive. Others fear mandating universal insurance coverage will increase taxes and insurance costs. Americans are also hesitant to see the government involved in an issue they believe should be market driven. They hold the Canadian system up as a negative example; they perceive it as having limited citizens' health-care choices and increased taxes and government bureaucracy.

Health-care reform became an important political topic in the 1990s. Government-sponsored health-care programs are an important factor in balancing the budget, and funding for such programs is threatened by rising costs. In general, politicians agreed the system should be fixed, but they could not agree on how. People disputed whether insurance costs for the poor should be provided primarily by the government, or "socialized"; provided by employers; or whether individuals should shop for their own through government-run or private agencies. In 1993, President Bill Clinton presented a plan for universal coverage. Employers would have had to provide health insurance for their employees. The unemployed would have received insurance through the government.

However, few liked Clinton's plan. The plan was over one thousand pages long and extremely complex; therefore, the majority of Americans and even the press had difficulty understanding it. Some feared it would dramatically change their current insurance. Business owners claimed that in the competitive world economy, mandates to provide insurance would limit their ability to compete; they said they would have to cut wages, cut jobs, or increase prices to cover insurance costs. And the American Medical Association, a lobbying group representing many of the nation's doctors, also opposed the plan, saying it would decrease the quality of care.

Several different groups and politicians put forth their own plans in response to the Clinton plan, but few could agree on the best way to reform the health-care system. Some states and businesses have started to reform health-care and insurance policies on their own. Even within the health-care system, market forces appear to be changing the system. For-profit health maintenance organizations (HMOs) have become more prevalent in the 1990s; they organize health-provider networks for large groups of customers, such as companies, for relatively low costs. But most attempts at reform still leave out the unemployed or part-time worker.

It took several decades of debate before Medicaid and Medicare were passed into law. Another nationwide attempt at health-care reform may take several more decades.

Related information: questions 34, 44

32 : *If you have a democratic constitution, why have your people had to fight for civil and equal rights?*

The U.S. Constitution is the oldest written constitution in the world that commits to democratic principles. However, it contains very broad principles of human freedom and rights that have been interpreted and implemented in different ways, depending on social and historical context. When the Constitution was written and adopted, for example, slavery was widely accepted. Women could not vote and had restricted rights to property ownership and education. So a struggle to refine laws to guarantee civil rights for *all* Americans has been taking place for more than two hundred years and will continue.

A series of laws, court rulings, and constitutional amendments has helped shape our country's practices relating to civil rights, but exactly what constitutes a civil right is still being debated. Does the constitutional right to "life, liberty, and the pursuit of happiness" include the right to hold a job? Does it include the right to government-provided health care? Does it include the right to receive government money to maintain a certain standard of living? These and other questions are still a matter of national debate.

Defining equal rights is particularly difficult in a pluralistic society like the United States's. When people do not come from equal backgrounds, it is difficult to ensure equal results or even equal opportunity. In response to demands from minorities, women, and people with physical disabilities, the government has succeeded over the last forty to fifty years in extending equal rights and equal protection under the law. But admittedly, we as a nation still have a long way to go. The fact that ethnic minorities make up most of the U.S. urban poor population indicates that Americans are not doing all they could to create equal opportunities. Women and minorities still face discrimination in the workplace, though such discrimination is illegal. And due in large part to limited local funds, public education in areas with large minority populations is not always equal to education offered elsewhere. Unequal educational opportunities eventually lead to disadvantages for minorities in the employment market.

Even so, how far U.S. policy should go to create opportunity for women and minorities is disputed. "Affirmative action" policies and programs have been in place in government agencies, schools, and businesses since the 1960s. These programs attempt to reverse past discrimination by giving preferential treatment to minority groups and women. Some specifically solicit applications from women and minorities or require that a certain percentage of employees or students come from a minority population. Advocates claim affirmative action simply helps women and minorities gain equal opportunities after centuries of discrimination. Opponents claim affirmative action programs cause reverse discrimination. The 1990s marked the thirty-year anniversary of many affirmative action policies and saw increased controversy over the effectiveness of such policies.

Certainly Americans will continue to struggle in defining, legislating, and implementing universal civil rights. The fact that no country has ever achieved a perfectly equal, democratic society points to the difficulties of the task.

Related information: questions 1, 38, 63

33 : *How can the American government—which protests human-rights violations in other countries—uphold capital punishment within its own borders?*

Whether or not the government's support of capital punishment is immoral and hypocritical is a controversial question even within the United States. From 1967 to 1976 executions were suspended while appellate courts and, eventually, the Supreme Court decided on the constitutionality of the death penalty. After many states modified their capital punishment laws, the Supreme Court ruled the laws constitutional. The first execution in ten years was carried out in 1977. Between 1977 and 1994, more than 250 additional executions were carried out, but in 1994, nearly three thousand prisoners sentenced to death were still awaiting execution.[13]

Every state has its own laws concerning capital crimes and punishment (twelve states still have no death penalty), but countrywide the

---

13. Tom Kuntz, "The Rage to Kill Those Who Kill," *New York Times*, Sunday, 4 December 1994, sec. 4.

number of prisoners on "death row" is growing. This growth is largely due to the fact that (1) all death sentences can be and usually are appealed a number of times and (2) rules governing appeals are inconsistent, very particular, and numerous, thus slowing the appeals process. To complicate matters, because laws are so complex and minute, the Supreme Court and lower courts have been contradictory in their rulings. For a death-penalty conviction to be overturned, a convict's sentence must be reversed on appeal (appellate courts automatically review cases resulting in death-penalty convictions), or the convict must be pardoned by the governor of his or her state.

What constitutes a capital crime has been disputed. In the past, rape was a capital crime, but the Supreme Court has ruled execution for a rape conviction "cruel and unusual punishment." Most death-row inmates today have been convicted of a murder they committed while committing another serious crime, such as robbery or rape.

Americans have strong feelings about capital punishment—pro or con. A get-tough-on-crime sentiment continues to grow in the United States, so it may not be surprising that a majority of Americans still favor capital punishment, for a variety of reasons. Most believe it is a fitting punishment for murder—that a murderer forfeits his or her right to live by taking another life. Some believe it makes sense economically; housing a prisoner for life who is guilty of a serious crime drains public resources that could be put to better use. Many believe the death penalty eliminates the possibility that dangerous criminals will return to the streets. Many think it deters crime: if someone knows they will die for taking a life, they may not kill. Those who believe capital punishment is a deterrent argue that court delays lessen the deterrent's effectiveness. They say the threat of capital punishment is a more effective deterrent if the punishment swiftly follows the crime.

The deterrent argument touches another issue. A few Americans who were sentenced to death were later proven innocent. However, proponents of capital punishment argue that even if a few innocent people are executed, the deterrent effects of capital punishment lead to fewer innocent lives being lost: fewer innocent victims are killed by the state than would be killed by murderers if murderers were not deterred by the threat of the death penalty.

Many of those who oppose capital punishment believe murder is morally wrong, even if administered by the government in a controlled setting. They argue that the judicial system is imperfect and that innocent people were executed in the past and might be in the future. And they say there is not enough evidence that the threat of execution actually deters crime. Capital punishment opponents claim pronouncing a death sentence is no more economical than housing prisoners, given the lengthy and costly appeals process. They say the government could better use its resources by helping reform criminals. A better policy, they believe, would be to allow criminals to live and, in some way, pay restitution (other than with their lives) to their victims' families. Finally, many opponents argue that the death penalty is discriminatory; for example, those who kill whites are more likely to be sentenced to death than those who kill blacks.

The United States is certainly not the only country dealing with this debate. Although most Western industrialized countries no longer practice capital punishment, many Asian, African, and Middle Eastern countries do. Whether or not capital punishment is "barbaric" is still contested, worldwide.

Related information: chapter 2 introduction

34 : *How does your government take care of your unemployed? your poor?*

Besides funding job-placement and job-training services, the U.S. government also provides monetary compensation to unemployed workers. U.S. laws require that most employers collect a tax on their employees' earnings as unemployment insurance. When workers lose their jobs involuntarily, they can then collect unemployment compensation for up to one year. More than 85 percent of workers are covered by this program.[14]

To help the poor, the government funds a variety of "welfare" programs. Perhaps the best known is Aid to Families with Dependent Children (AFDC), which provides money for children who live in single-parent homes and their guardians. Other programs offer funds to those affected by an emergency that limits their abilities to meet basic needs, and there are programs that help the elderly and disabled.

Additional forms of government aid include Social Security, meant to subsidize elderly Americans' pensions; Medicaid, offering health insurance for the poor, and Medicare, offering health insurance to the elderly; food stamps, which low-income families can trade for food; subsidized school meals for children from low-income families; subsidized housing; and more. To provide short-term solutions to the problems of homelessness and hunger, state and city governments help fund private shelters and soup kitchens for the needy.

Costs for welfare programs have increased tremendously over the last several decades and have sparked debate over the efficacy of certain programs. As teenage birth rates and single parenthood have increased, AFDC has become particularly controversial. Conservative Americans, who are advocates of individual effort, argue that welfare programs such as AFDC foster dependency and encourage out-of-wedlock births. More liberal Americans, who typically advocate social planning, are in favor of continuing to offer aid. For the most part, members of both groups agree that the welfare system should remain in place but should be restructured to discourage dependency.

The government has made attempts at reform. A 1988 law requires that people on welfare, with children over three years of age, participate in job-training and educational programs. In the 1990s, politicians have proposed that disincentives in the present system be done away with.

---

14. *The New Grolier Multimedia Encyclopedia,* CD-ROM release 6, s.v. "unemployment insurance."

For example, currently welfare money is cut if a single mother gets married, and a teenage mother continues to receive money if she drops out of school. Some have proposed not cutting funding to those who marry and not funding a young woman to leave her parents' home and drop out of school. Some have also argued against continually increasing payments for women who have a number of children out of wedlock. But many believe some of these strategies would only hurt children.

Others suggest that increasing the government's power to collect "support" money from absent fathers would help single mothers. Another suggested reform is to eliminate national welfare programs and allow states to determine how best to help their needy.

Hard choices lie ahead for Americans as both social problems and the national deficit continue to increase. Decisions about how to change and fund programs are imperative, but controversy surrounding those decisions appears inevitable.

Related information: questions 10, 31

35 : *How do you get your people to pay taxes? Why are your taxes so much lower than ours?*

Though critical of government waste, Americans, in general, feel obliged to pay their share of taxes.[15] Most attempt to minimize their tax payments, but only a minority attempt to avoid paying them altogether. So, apart from the fact that the U.S. government provides fewer services than other governments, U.S. taxes are lower than taxes in other countries precisely because Americans generally comply with tax laws.

The government gets the majority of its funds from direct taxes, including individual income tax; corporate income tax; Social Security

---

15. The following served as a general source for the information contained in this response: Robert J. Samuelson, "We Are Not a Nation of Tax Cheats," *Newsweek* 123, no. 15 (11 April 1994): 58.

tax, which funds subsidies for retirees' pensions and other social programs; payroll tax, which funds unemployment compensation; and property tax, which funds community services such as education, libraries, parks, and police. Other government funds come through indirect taxes, including sales and excise taxes on goods and services.

Several factors keep Americans in taxpaying compliance. First, the government's direct methods of collection help ensure that it receives tax payments. A 1913 amendment to the U.S. Constitution allowed the government to collect income tax, but it wasn't until World War II that the government began withholding income taxes from employees' wages. Payroll taxes and Social Security taxes are also automatically withheld from workers' pay. Even self-employed Americans have to pay taxes throughout the year based on their estimated income.

This has proven to be a highly effective collection method. The employer estimates the amount of tax a worker will need to pay and withholds that amount from workers' paychecks, so wage earners are able to pay as they go. Before mid-April of each year, workers have to reconcile their account with the government. If the tax collected is less than the amount owed, they have to pay the government the difference. If the tax collected is more than the amount owed, they receive money back from the government. The government attempts to keep tax forms and the payment process simple enough that people will be inclined to fill out forms and pay.

Another factor that motivates Americans to pay is the threat of tax-law enforcement. The Internal Revenue Service (IRS), the government agency that collects taxes, has the power to track people's revenue and spending, to verify that they are paying taxes in proportion to their income. That power has been enhanced in recent years by computer technology. The fear of being monitored and audited by the IRS keeps many Americans in compliance.

In addition, Americans are willing to pay taxes because U.S. taxes are relatively low. Many Americans would disagree with that statement, but compared to Europeans and other citizens around the world, Americans pay a smaller amount of their total national income in local, state, and federal taxes combined—about 30 percent. Other countries have combined tax rates closer to 40, 50, and even 60 percent of their national income. The U.S. government has tried to strike a balance between too-high taxes, which would seem to generate revenue but would increase tax evasion, and too-low taxes, which would not create enough revenue but would encourage payment.

Americans are also willing to comply with tax laws because they perceive laws as being fair. The rich are expected to pay more, and the poor are expected to pay less.

Certainly tax collecting in the United States can become a contest between (1) people's attempts, legal and illegal, to avoid or reduce tax payments and (2) the government's ability to collect taxes and find ways to prevent people from cheating, underreporting their income, and underpaying. But overall, the United States has been more effective in collecting taxes than many other countries. Meanwhile the U.S. Congress continues to pass laws to strengthen tax-law enforcement. Over the last decade, politicians and economists have discussed whether the United States should adopt the value-added tax implemented in Europe. However, most Americans resist such a tax; many say that, with the relatively high compliance rate in the United States, such a tax is not needed.

36 : *What role does religion play in American politics?*

The relationship between religion and U.S. politics is a complex one. The U.S. Constitution outlines a society wherein matters of church and government should be separate. It specifically states that Congress should make no law "respecting an establishment of religion, or prohibiting the free exercise thereof." For the most part, an admirable separation between church and state has been maintained. There is no state-supported church, churches enjoy certain protections to worship as they please, and public institutions—such as schools—are protected under law from the undue influence of churches. But there is always overlap.

Basic Judeo-Christian values and morals are the foundation of many Constitutional principles and U.S. laws. The government also passes laws that some Americans believe to be an offense to basic Judeo-Christian values and teachings. Conversely, churches teach doctrines that influence their members' political views. Churches sometimes even exercise political power by lobbying for or publicly opposing certain legislation.

Throughout history, religious beliefs have shaped political debates and movements. Not surprisingly, issues that evoke religious arguments have tended to be the most controversial. Slavery, temperance, civil rights, abortion, and capital punishment are just a few political topics that have elicited arguments from different religious viewpoints—pro and con.

Although religion influences political movements and individuals' political views, U.S. politicians—as public representatives—generally do not allow their religious beliefs to completely define their political stances. Only a small number of politicians who have overtly preached their particular religious beliefs have remained popular and in office, especially in the latter part of the twentieth century.

In the 1960 presidential election campaign, John F. Kennedy's Catholic faith was a major issue. Up to that point, U.S. presidents had affiliated with a variety of Protestant religions. However, Kennedy assured voters that the Catholic clergy would not dictate his decisions, and while in office he demonstrated that his religion did not necessarily define his political positions. His presidency alleviated the fears of many Americans that a president's religion would dominate the office. Most Americans now acknowledge that religion plays a role in shaping political attitudes but is not definitive.

Still, some of today's leading political movements are influenced by religion. In the 1980s and 1990s, the politically conservative, Christian "Religious Right" movement has grown in popularity. Religious Right supporters believe social problems, such as increased crime and teenage pregnancy, are the result of Americans adopting moral relativity and liberal permissiveness. They believe that, instead of government programs, a rebuilding of community structures, such as the family and church, would help an ailing American society.

The liberal side of U.S. politics, or "left," is less known for its explicitly religious views. But a "Religious Left" does exist. This group has traditionally called for more government intervention relating to minority rights and needs, i.e., desegregation, affirmative action, socioeconomic equality and development, and civil rights. Notable among the "left" are African-American Baptists, some Jewish intellectuals, and Catholic leaders who promote social development. Martin Luther King Jr. and Jesse Jackson have been key leaders in this political movement.

Thus, even though the U.S. Constitution calls for a separation of church and state, religion does influence U.S. politics. Understandably, most Americans find it difficult to completely separate their religious beliefs from their political opinions.

37 : *Is it true that your government funds abortion? How do Americans feel about that?*

In 1973, the Supreme Court ruled in one of the most controversial and divisive cases in U.S. history: *Roe v. Wade.* The court ruled against a state law that prohibited abortion. It decided that states cannot forbid a woman's right to abortion during the first three months of pregnancy and can only forbid abortion in the second three months under certain circumstances—if the fetus is capable of surviving outside the womb and if the mother's life or health are not in danger. (More than a decade later, the Court found that states may require doctors to determine, through tests, whether or not a fetus might survive outside the womb.) The Court determined that the decision to have an abortion is a privacy issue.

After this decision was announced, the federal government and some state governments funded abortions for women who qualified for Medicaid—government-funded health insurance for the poor. The Supreme Court eventually ruled that the government was not obligated to fund all abortions: states could place limits on federal funds allocated for abortions. However, the federal government has since limited states' freedom to choose which abortions they will provide Medicaid funds for. Still, states continue to argue for the right to determine the nature of abortion funding within their borders.

Americans are strongly divided not only on the issue of funding abortions but on the entire premise of legal abortion. The issue is complicated, but the controversy involves two basic issues: "choice" and "life." As to choice, some Americans believe that a woman should have the right to make decisions regarding her body and that her rights supersede the rights of an unborn fetus whose "humanity" is in question. They believe that trying to legislate against legal abortion is an attempt by male politicians to exercise control over women's rights to choose. These people call themselves "pro-choice." Others believe that life and "humanity" begins at conception and, therefore, that aborting a fetus is equivalent to killing a human being. Government sanctioning of abortion, they believe, sets a dangerous precedent for the disregard of the sanctity of human life. These people call themselves "pro-life."

The names and arguments adopted by each side are not entirely accurate. The term "pro-life" implies that those who are "pro-choice" believe in death; however, most pro-choice advocates believe abortion is not death or murder because the humanity of the fetus is in question. They argue that the point where life—and the fetus's rights—begins is unclear. The term "pro-choice" implies that pro-life advocates do not believe in choice for women. In fact, many who are pro-life believe women do have a right to choose; however, when women choose to engage in sexual activity, they also choose the consequence of pregnancy. Some pro-life advocates also believe that those who did not exercise free choice in their pregnancy—such as victims of incest or rape or women whose lives may be in danger—should have a choice about whether they abort the child or not.

Pro-life advocates are morally opposed to abortion and government funding of it. Pro-choice advocates believe public funds should be provided for abortion—just as they are for other health-care procedures. They feel that if abortions are not funded, women, and particularly young, low-income women, will have abortions through unsafe means or will bear unwanted children.

Unfortunately, the debate has led to violence in recent years. Pro-life demonstrators have blocked entrances to abortion clinics. A few pro-life supporters have even killed abortion doctors and abortion-clinic workers and patrons in isolated incidences of violence. These actions have led to federal law guaranteeing access to abortion clinics and limiting demonstrations.

Because this issue involves strongly held fundamental beliefs about choice and life, the debate about government involvement in abortion will continue in the United States and in American politics.

38 : *What role does the U.S. government play in organizing and financing your educational system?*

Since the early days of U.S. history, schools have been regarded as local institutions. The U.S. Constitution does not mention education explicitly, and its Tenth Amendment declares that powers not delegated to the federal government by the Constitution are reserved to the states or to the people. Funding structures reflect the fact that states and citizens are largely responsible for the U.S. educational system. During the 1987–88 year, 50 percent of public-school funds came from states, 44 percent from local sources, and only 6 percent from the federal government.[16]

Indeed, the U.S. educational system is marked by an absence of national, centralized control. The federal government includes a De-

---

16. *The New Grolier Multimedia Encyclopedia*, CD-ROM release 6, s.v. "United States, education in the."

partment of Education, whose secretary serves as one of the president's official advisors—as part of his cabinet—but the department's function is not to vigilantly supervise schools in the fifty states. Instead, it performs a variety of functions aimed at increasing the quality of education and the equality of educational opportunity nationwide.

The department funds research on national educational issues, collects data and statistics, and issues reports on findings. It also provides states with unrestricted "block grants" and grants for specific programs. Most of these programs target specific groups of Americans: preparing economically and educationally disadvantaged children for public schooling, providing educational support for veterans, subsidizing school meals for needy children, etc. The department also supports the development of educational programs in fields that are underfunded—e.g., science, math, foreign-language, and vocational education. In addition, the federal government offsets post-secondary tuition costs in the form of student grants and low-interest student loans. In short, the Department of Education's main functions are examining national educational issues and meeting specific needs of targeted populations.

States are generally regarded as the centers of educational control. State administrators, including the state board and superintendent of education, are elected or appointed. They establish educational standards in several areas—competency standards for various grades, length of school year, curriculum, school buildings, texts, teacher certification, etc.—and they monitor compliance. State administrators may also help determine how federal grants are distributed. State legislatures are involved in allocating state funds for education and in making policy regarding certain issues, such as the licensing of teachers. States financially support and supervise public universities and colleges as well as primary and secondary schools. They also indirectly control private schools by setting statewide curricular and other standards.

If states have regulatory control, local school "districts" control implementation of standards and operations. The United States contains more than ten thousand school districts, which encompass geographic regions of varying sizes within a state.[17] Each district has a school board (again either elected or appointed) that appoints a superintendent of local schools. These administrators help direct and supervise local operations and ensure that schools within district boundaries implement state regulations.

The democratic ideal behind the vast U.S. public educational system is that everyone will have an equal opportunity for education. The system is fairly uniform in structure, but because funding and implementation decisions are controlled mainly at state and local levels, schools are not necessarily uniform in curriculum content or in funding.

The issue of educational funding is becoming increasingly controversial. Local property taxes provide the bulk of public school funds in many areas. Therefore, poorer areas have less money to fund schools. Poorer areas also tend to have more social problems, such as teenage pregnancy, crime, and lack of community support for education. So not only do schools not have adequate funds for educational programs, they also lack funds to overcome "extracurricular" social problems. Because schools do not help meet the needs of many poor students, these students often leave school. They lack job skills, they remain poor, and their children follow the same educational path. Thus, the democratic ideal of equal opportunity is not achieved in many areas. Some even argue that inequitable funding violates the "equal protection of the laws" clause of the U.S. Constitution's Fourteenth Amendment.

In 1971, a three-judge federal panel in the state of Texas found that the state was violating the Constitution's equal protection clause precisely because its system of funding, based on local property taxes, resulted in highly unequal school districts. Two years later, however, the U.S. Supreme Court reversed the decision, stating that discrepancies in school funding did not violate the Constitution and that the issue should

---

17. *Encyclopedia Americana*, 1995 International ed., s.v. "Education: 9. Educational Administration."

be addressed by state officials.[18] Some twenty years later, the issue is still being argued in courts throughout the country. During the 1990s, the Texas Supreme Court has upheld a plan to make the state's wealthiest school districts share several hundred million dollars' worth of property tax revenues with poorer districts.

Many other states are debating how to better provide for their schools. Some states, like Texas, now redistribute school funds through state tax levies to ameliorate funding disparities between rich and poor areas. In 1993, the Michigan state legislature abolished the practice of relying on local property taxes to support school budgets. Citizens voted to fund education through higher sales and cigarette taxes and other levies. The state also placed a spending cap on wealthier school districts and a minimum spending limit for schools in poorer districts. (Spending before was widely disparate: a $7,000 difference existed in per-pupil spending between the wealthiest and poorest districts.) States around the country will be watching to see if this new funding plan is effective.

During the 1990s, a few school districts undertook another innovative tactic that will be closely monitored. These districts turned their management over to private companies in an effort to balance their budgets and better their educational outcomes, such as student completion rates and test scores. If private companies help these school districts, privatization of school districts nationwide might increase.

Related information: questions 6, 32

18. *San Antonio Independent School District v Rodriguez.*

CHAPTER THREE

THREE

AMERICA

IN THE

WORLD ECONOMY

The collapse of the Soviet Union and the end of the Cold War have created an entirely new situation for U.S. foreign and national security policy. (See chapter four introduction.) Economically, however, the world remains the same in many ways. Two major issue areas still dominate U.S. participation in the world economy. The first is trade and economic relations with developed, economically mature countries. Generally speaking, the more developed a country is, the more extensive the trade and economic relationship it has with other developed countries, including the United States. The issues that arise for the United States in dealing with other developed countries are coping with the growing internationalization of business and undertaking steps to increase trade by removing impediments to freer economic relations.

The second issue area involves U.S. economic relations with developing countries. During the Cold War, the economic issues that dominated relations between the develop*ed* countries (which were primarily in the northern hemisphere) and develop*ing* countries (which were primarily in the southern hemisphere) were dubbed "North-South" issues. This label distinguished them from "East-West" issues, involving the United States and Western Europe (the "West") and the Soviet Union and Eastern Europe (the "East"). Although East-West issues are no longer relevant, North-South issues are. The United States, western Europe, and Japan have common interests that differ from the interests of developing countries in Asia, Africa, Latin America, and the former eastern bloc.

Knowing the perspective of your non-American questioner is important in answering questions about economic issues. People from western Europe and Japan are likely to share a similar point of view about the role of government in the economy, and they are likely to understand and appreciate free-market forces. Their economic perspective is probably closer to ours. Individuals from developing countries approach economic issues from a somewhat different perspective. In most of these countries economic development is a national priority, and the government is actively and intimately involved in encouraging the development of targeted sectors of economic activity. Foreign trade is not unhindered, left to be guided principally by supply and demand; generally, the government carefully manages trade to maximize economic development.

Relating to the first major issue area—U.S. economic relations with developed countries—a major concern of the United States and other developed countries is coping with the expanding internationalization of business. Increasingly the products Americans purchase—clothing, electronic equipment, automobiles, gasoline, even food—are made, grown, and/or extracted abroad. At the same time, more of the products Americans grow or manufacture are shipped to consumers abroad. Corporations are increasingly international in their outlook. Businesspeople travel and live in many countries. The manager of the northern California region for a major American hotel corporation is a Frenchman, while the manager of the company's Budapest hotel is a non-Hungarian-speaking American. Corporations increasingly make decisions on the basis of international markets. For an American electronics company, deciding where to build its newest production facility does not simply involve the question of whether to build in California's Silicon Valley or along Massachusetts's Route 128; the issue is Ireland versus Singapore versus Taiwan versus the Czech Republic versus an American site.

As the world economy becomes increasingly international rather than national in focus, serious problems emerge for national governments that attempt to regulate the businesses operating within their boundaries. With the growth of computer use, the ease of electronic funds transfers, and the ease of international communications via telephone, fax, computer modems, and electronic mail, governments are finding it ever more difficult to monitor the workings of businesses—even those that are ostensibly headquartered within the country. International banking and business scandals have highlighted the problems national governments face in controlling fraud and other illegal activities, as well as simply knowing what is taking place within their borders. The Bank of Credit and Commerce International (BCCI) was owned principally by wealthy individuals in Abu Dhabi, managed by a Pakistani, incorporated in Luxembourg and the Cayman Islands, and had major banking operations in Britain, the United States, and many other developed countries. The scandal, which ultimately caused the shutdown of BCCI in 1991, was investigated by government regulators from a dozen countries.

The same forces that have permitted the expansion of international business have also permitted the expansion and internationalization of crime, which has become a growing concern of national governments as well as a burden on consumers and legitimate businesses around the world. Large organized criminal businesses operate much as any lawful international business, with many legitimate activities used to launder and reinvest illicit profits. The American and Italian Mafia, Colombian drug cartels, and Asian criminal enterprises are only a few examples. One rising international concern is the growth of the so-called Russian Mafia, whose activities have principally focused on internal activities in Russia but show disturbing signs of developing international criminal ties. The burden of such criminal activities falls on everyone. Tax evasion increases the tax burden for those who pay their fair share of government costs. Drug use, which is abetted and encouraged by drug cartels, imposes a heavy social, moral, and financial burden on American and European cities, driving up costs of law enforcement and medical care. Bribery of public officials distorts government procurement and public policy. "Pirating" software does not give a fair return to developers, which discourages further development efforts; pirating video and audio performances denies the original producers their fair return as well. Just as governments have had to increasingly regulate legitimate businesses in a world that is becoming more interconnected, the internationalization of crime has created additional, serious costs for society and burdens for governments.

Now that the economy is truly international, economic forces such as international supply and demand are more important than political forces. A national government's policies have always played a key role in the national economy and in trade, but since national economies have become more involved in the world economy, it is considerably more difficult and complex for government policies to influence a national economy. This perspective is important in considering questions about the U.S. economy and its role in the world economy.

In the area of U.S. economic relations with developed, economically mature countries, another major concern of the United States is dealing with barriers to trade. The United States has the largest economy in the world by a substantial margin.[1] Although making numerical comparisons is not an exact science, the numbers present an interesting picture. In 1996, the United States will have an economy that produces $7.4 trillion in goods and services. The second largest economy, Japan, will produce about $5.3 trillion. Third in size is Germany at a level of $2.3 trillion, followed by France at $1.5 trillion, and Britain and Italy at $1.2 trillion.[2] Because of its sheer size, the U.S. economy has a substantial impact on the rest of the world. Non-American questioners, from

---

1. Comparing national economies is a particularly difficult task because of fundamental differences in the nature of each country's economy and because comparisons are expressed in a common unit (U.S. dollars), which distorts relationships since the value of national currencies fluctuates and is skewed by trade and international finance issues.

2. Louis S. Richman, "Global Growth Is on a Tear," *Fortune* 131, no. 5 (20 March 1995): 108.

developed and developing countries, may both admire the economic success the United States has enjoyed and resent its economic influence on the rest of the world.

Because the U.S. economy is so large, however, the volume of U.S. international trade is proportionately smaller than that of some other countries. In 1993, the European Union (Germany, France, Britain, Italy, Spain, Denmark, Greece, Portugal, Belgium, the Netherlands, Luxembourg, and Ireland) had a combined population one-third larger than the United States's, an economy that was only seven-eighths as large as the United States's, but combined exports and imports that were almost three times the value of total U.S. trade.[3] Because of the size and sophistication of its national economy, however, the United States is significantly involved in international trade and has a significant impact on the world economy.

Both Republican and Democratic presidents have generally followed policies encouraging freer, more open trade. The United States was a major force pressing for the 1994 Uruguay Round agreements to liberalize trade worldwide under the General Agreement on Tariffs and Trade (GATT). In 1988, Canada and the United States approved a free trade agreement between the two countries. And in 1993, that agreement was expanded to include Mexico with the United States and Canada in the North American Free Trade Agreement (NAFTA).

Although U.S. policy attempted to expand trade generally, Americans have had particular concerns that reflect the nature of our economy and the kinds of products we export. The United States exports a substantial amount of agricultural goods, due to the fertility of its farm areas and the efficiency of its agriculture industry. As a result, the United States has pressed the European Union (EU) for the removal of subsidies on EU agricultural products. Since products of the American entertain-

---

3. Central Intelligence Agency, Directorate of Intelligence, "Table 2. Selected OECD Countries: Economic Profile, 1993," in *Handbook of Economic Statistics: 1994*, CPAS 94–10001 (Wash., D.C.: Central Intelligence Agency, 1994), 16.

ment industry make up such a significant part of overall export earnings, the U.S. government has strongly opposed foreign governments' efforts to restrict foreign content on television and in movies. Another key issue for U.S. trade has been "intellectual property": the research, development, and intellectual effort invested in production of such items as computer programs, films, music, books, and other materials that are copyrighted and patented. The main concern of U.S. government and business has been the sale of "pirated" versions of such American products.

While the United States fostered open trade to permit free-market forces to determine products and trade flows, U.S. policy has been somewhat inconsistent. Even as the United States has opposed government intervention in trade and urged reduction of tariffs, it has also been adamant in pressing the Japanese government to adopt policies that will help expand U.S. exports to Japan. The U.S. trade deficit with Japan has been particularly significant and persistent. For example, in 1994 the deficit was $65 billion, and during the first four months of 1995 it stood at more than $21 billion.[4] To deal with that problem, the United States has engaged periodically in high-stakes confrontations involving threatened retaliation in the form of punitive U.S. tariffs on some Japanese products. The United States has argued that Japanese wholesale practices, the vertical integration of the domestic Japanese market, and interrelationships between Japanese cartels have excluded U.S. companies from fair access to the Japanese market. The American complaints have a certain validity, but the tactics used by the Reagan, Bush, and Clinton administrations have caused some consternation in Europe and elsewhere. Despite other countries' tacit support for U.S. efforts to open the Japa-

---

4. U.S. Department of Commerce, Bureau of the Census/Bureau of Economic Analysis, "Exhibit 13. Exports, Imports and Trade Balance by Country and Area, Not Seasonally Adjusted: 1994," in *U.S. International Trade in Goods and Services: Annual Revision for 1994* (Wash., D.C.: Government Printing Office, 21 June 1995), 20; U.S. Department of Commerce, Bureau of the Census/Bureau of Economic Analysis, "Exhibit 14. Exports, Imports and Trade Balance by Country and Area—1994," in *U.S. International Trade*, 19.

nese market, the unilateral threat of trade sanctions contrasts sharply with general American support for freer trade.

Within the United States, the efforts of various administrations to promote reduced tariffs and freer trade have not been universally supported. During the first 150 years of America's existence as a nation, business interests and the Republican Party (after its founding) generally supported protective tariffs, believing they benefited American industry, while organized labor and the Democratic party supported reduced tariffs and freer trade.

In the past decades, these positions have been reversed. American business now generally favors more open trade and reduced tariffs, as long as American business has access to foreign markets under the same open rules. U.S. business wants the ability to manufacture where labor costs are lowest and to sell anywhere, including the American market. American-designed products are now produced in Taiwan, Hong Kong, China, Singapore, India, and throughout Europe. Organized labor in the United States has seen manufacturing jobs migrate to other countries where low-cost labor is available, particularly for production of textiles/clothing, shoes, and electronics. As a result, labor unions have increasingly and with greater vigor opposed agreements such as the Uruguay Round of GATT and NAFTA in an effort to protect American jobs. Labor and its supporters in Congress have pressed for legislation to restrict trade, such as "Buy American" laws that limit the U.S. government to purchasing products that have a minimum component "made in the U.S.A."

An ongoing debate in the United States about using national trade and tariff policies for noneconomic policy purposes has focused on most-favored-nation status (MFN). Granting MFN status means granting another country the lowest tariff rate or "most favored" treatment in its trade with the United States. This concept dates back to the era of bilateral trade agreements between two countries, but among developed nations with market economies, it has been replaced by multinational agreements under GATT. However, countries with nonmarket economies (basically, communist countries) are not able to participate in GATT, and bilateral trade arrangements still prevail.

In the early 1970s, as the United States was trying to improve relations with the Soviet Union under the Richard Nixon-Henry Kissinger policy of détente, the United States considered extending MFN status to the Soviet Union. Under congressional pressure and eventually legislation, MFN status was not granted to nonmarket countries unless they permitted free immigration—a stipulation expanded (in the popular and congressional perception, though not in legislative language) to include respect for fundamental human rights. Granting MFN status to the Soviet Union remained an issue in U.S.-Soviet relations until the collapse of the USSR. With the end of communist regimes in the former USSR and Eastern Europe, countries in these regions have become participants in GATT, and MFN is no longer an issue.

It remains a concern with China, however. The president has the authority to extend MFN on a temporary basis for twelve months at a time to nonmarket countries if Congress does not act to block the action. MFN has been extended to China for a number of years by presidents of both parties, but following the Chinese government's brutal suppression of a pro-democracy student movement in Beijing's Tiananmen Square in June 1989, congressional critics of China's human-rights policy have repeatedly called for withdrawal of MFN status. The issue is fought annually when the president decides whether to extend MFN for another year. The arguments against MFN for China emphasize the importance of "giving teeth" to our support for human rights. Those in support of MFN argue the importance of our trade links with China and suggest that encouraging economic expansion in China will lead to economic and political reform in the long run. The broader question of using trade and economic pressure for our foreign policy purposes is an ongoing debate in the United States that is far from resolved.

The second broad issue area regarding U.S. participation in the world economy involves U.S. economic relations with developing countries.

Non-Americans from these countries are likely to ask very different kinds of questions than those from developed countries.

Individuals from developing countries are likely to perceive a fundamental unfairness in international economic relations. This perception has some basis in fact. The world's economic resources are not equitably divided. The United States, with some 260 million people, has the world's largest economy. China, with a population almost five times larger than that of the United States, has an economy that is less than one-tenth the size of the U.S. economy. India, with a population three and one-half times the size of the United States's, has an economy that is only about one-twentieth the size. Canada, with a population of about twenty-nine million people, only about one-fortieth the size of China, has an economy that is almost as large as China's.[5]

Furthermore, Americans consume a disproportionate share of the world's resources. Our energy consumption per capita is more than twice that of Japan, and we consume almost twice as much energy as the developed European countries. We contribute a disproportionate share to the world's pollution: American industries spew into the atmosphere twice the amount of carbon dioxide per capita as industries in Japan and the developed European countries.

Some also see an unfairness in the distribution of natural resources. This view is not due simply to the objective fact that some countries are blessed with abundant natural wealth, while others are particularly barren. One need only look at Saudi Arabia, Kuwait, Iraq, Iran, and Libya, with their considerable wealth in oil and natural gas, to understand that truth. However, some non-Americans believe developed countries conspire—consciously or unconsciously—to undervalue the resources and products that developing countries have or produce (with the obvious exception of oil and natural gas). Some intellectuals from these countries feel their countries are exploited and argue that developed countries, including the United States, extract resources from developing countries at

5. Central Intelligence Agency, Directorate of Intelligence, "Table 2."

unfavorably low prices and then sell industrial products at an inordinately high value. While there is no conspiracy, individuals from developing countries, who are accustomed to considerable government involvement in national economic development, may approach this question from a perspective that would lead them to such a conclusion.

In fact, there is nothing more sinister at work than the fundamental economic forces of supply and demand. The U.S. policies discussed above—dealing with the internationalization of business and the long-term effort to reduce barriers to trade—are all intended to permit the factors of competition to have greater effect. Almost all Americans possess a fundamental belief in the value of the free market and favor policies that will allow free-market forces to work. Americans' commitment to market economics underlies their support for the extensive economic reforms taking place in Russia, other republics of the former Soviet Union, and central and eastern Europe. Trade relations with communist China are in part justified by the argument that the economic transformation taking place there, and the links between China and the world economy, are producing political changes that will ultimately bring China to the path Russia is now following.

39 : *Has economic nationalism replaced anticommunism in American thinking? Hasn't America been increasingly resorting to economic nationalism, which borders on xenophobia, particularly toward Japan?*

Some have called the pervading atmosphere after the end of the Cold War a kind of "capitalist cold war."[6] They argue that Americans are now eager for protectionism in an economic rather than in a military sense—

---

6. The following served as a general source for the information contained in this response: John T. Rourke, *International Politics on the World Stage*, 4th ed. (Guilford, Conn.: Dushkin Publishing Group, 1993), 72–73, 178, 466–67.

that they want protection, not from a communist political takeover, but from an economic takeover, particularly by Japan. They say Americans' fear of Japanese economic power has grown in direct proportion to their decreasing fear of Soviet nuclear power.

This argument may be true—to an extent. Since the end of the Cold War, Americans have turned much of their attention to domestic, especially economic, issues. They are highly concerned about the already large U.S. trade deficit. Many supporters of economic nationalism see the further opening of markets to foreign trade as giving away U.S. jobs and sovereignty. However, the majority of U.S. economists and politicians forecast that the United States will have to engage in more free-trade agreements to compete in the world market. They say the United States has to protect its interests, but economic nationalism is not viable. Indeed, the United States's signing of the North American Free Trade Agreement and other regional and global trade agreements in the 1990s indicates the U.S. government does not see economic nationalism as a viable stance.

As for xenophobia, Americans could be described as being xenophobic toward Japan. Studies show the majority of Americans have friendly feelings toward the Japanese,[7] but economically, the Japanese make us feel somewhat insecure, and so we fear them. That fear may be purely racial in some cases, but it is more likely based on Americans' perceptions of a "superior" Japanese business sense. Over the last few decades, Americans have heard a great deal about the success of Japan's schools and its highly disciplined workforce. And when Japanese direct investment in U.S. ventures increased in the 1980s, journalists reported that the Japanese were "buying up America."

However, those fears were largely unfounded. The sheer size of the U.S. economy means foreign investment accounts for only a small percentage of private enterprise, and Europeans have a larger share in that

7. Data taken from a New York Times/CBS News poll conducted 5–7 October 1991, cited in Rourke, *International Politics*, 131.

small percentage than do the Japanese. In addition, Japanese investment in U.S. enterprises fell during the 1990s because of the expansion of investment opportunities in Asia and the recession in the United States.

Another possible reason for Americans' xenophobia or distrust of the Japanese is that some feel the Japanese do not play fairly when it comes to trade. Japanese trade restrictions have limited U.S. agricultural, automotive, and other imports in the past, and higher prices imposed through Japanese tariffs have reduced the competitiveness of U.S. products in Japan. However, trade agreements reached in the 1990s have decreased Japanese protectionist measures and will likely continue to do so.

The transition to a world economy will require time and adjustments by all members of the global community. Americans are accustomed to being "in charge." The Japanese are accustomed to protections for certain industries. Perhaps as these trade partners adjust to new roles and rules in working out trade issues, there will be less animosity between them—either real or perceived.

Related information: question 43

40 : *Why does America place so much emphasis on free trade? Does your country simply want a stronger position than its trading partners to exploit them?*

It is true that the United States places emphasis on free trade because it expects to benefit from it. However, free trade is generally recognized as benefiting all countries involved.

Free trade means lower tariffs and other protectionist measures, which bring several advantages. Export sales expand not only because prices on exports decrease (through lower tariffs) but because incomes—and thus buying power—abroad increase. Expanded export sales also mean more jobs available at home. Prices on imports are lower. And increased competition between more countries also leads to lower prices and better quality goods. Some even say that if countries are bound together through equitable free-trade agreements, they will cooperate in other areas, and political tensions between countries will diminish.

Unless a smaller country's exports are identical to a larger country's exports (and, therefore, the smaller country is in direct competition with the larger country) the smaller country will benefit from free trade. In fact, smaller countries are more likely to benefit than larger ones, such as the United States. They gain access to a greater variety of goods than before, and the world market prices for the goods they sell will likely be so much higher than their production prices that they can undersell larger countries and still gain substantial profits.

In light of the question, it is ironic that many Americans fear free trade will put the United States in a weaker trade position in relation to its partners. Just as many in Third World countries fear they will be overrun by industrialized countries through free trade, some Americans believe their borders will be overrun. They believe reducing tariffs, quotas, and other protectionist measures will mean jobs and capital flooding out of the country and cheap imports flooding in. Americans have complained that by entering into agreements such as the North American Free Trade Agreement and organizations such as the World Trade Organization they give up their right to be self-directing in trade and political matters. Thus, many believe the United States is "weakened" and "exploited" by opening up to free trade, just as many smaller nations believe they are weakened and exploited.

In reality, all countries should benefit from free trade. Some countries may benefit more than others. And some groups within a country will benefit more than others—some groups may even be worse off—but overall we will all be better off.

Related information: questions 41, 42

41 : *If free trade is so good, why aren't my neighbors and I better off under free trade than before?*

While free trade benefits all countries, on average, there are some sectors within countries that may be worse off. Jobs related to certain industries will be lost. For example, U.S. textile workers, citrus and sugar farmers, and furniture makers are expected to suffer some job loss under the North American Free Trade Agreement (NAFTA). These industries, among others, will face tough competition from Mexican industries. On the other hand, U.S. grain farmers and machinery manufacturers will likely gain from markets opening in Mexico under NAFTA. So not all industries—or industry workers—receive equal benefits under free trade.

In addition, reaping the benefits of free-trade agreements takes time. Under NAFTA, tariffs and other restrictions will be lowered or removed over as many as fifteen years. So it may be some time before citizens feel the full effects of the free-trade agreements their countries sign.

Related information: questions 40, 42

42 : *Why does the United States send such mixed signals on free trade?*

While the average U.S. citizen will be better off under free trade, groups of workers in some industries may be hurt by it. These groups pressure politicians to fight against free-trade agreements such as the North American Free Trade Agreement (NAFTA) and the Uruguay Round of the General Agreement on Tariffs and Trade (GATT). Politicians depend on their constituents to remain in office and, therefore, may oppose free-trade legislation to support their constituents' interests. So while many U.S. citizens and politicians advocate free trade, others strongly oppose it.

For example, the U.S. textile industry knew it would lose business to overseas competitors with the 1994 GATT agreement, which lowered tariffs and other barriers on imported textiles. Representatives of the textile industry pressured politicians from their states to vote against the agreement. One influential U.S. senator from a textile state succeeded in slowing ratification of the agreement in Congress, although it eventually passed.

Other Americans pressure politicians to oppose free-trade agreements for different reasons. Some believe involvement with international organizations such as the World Trade Organization (WTO) will jeopardize U.S. political sovereignty. Others fear there will be a "giant sucking sound" south of the United States—that jobs and capital will leave the United States for developing nations.

Some Americans with humanitarian concerns worry that companies will leave the United States, which has strict workers'-rights laws, simply to exploit foreign workers. Environmentalists fear that free-trade agreements will lead to misuse of natural resources in less-developed countries. They believe industries will move to areas where environmental standards are low and monitoring of laws is lax. Many Americans simply think the "old way" of conducting trade—limiting imports and subsidizing exports—is still the best way. Protectionist and nationalistic feelings especially tend to flare during recessions and economic hard times.

Proponents of free trade pressure politicians to support more liberal trade agreements. They argue that U.S. involvement in organizations such as the WTO will not jeopardize U.S. sovereignty because WTO policies cannot overturn U.S. law. And although each country has one vote, the United States can exercise its leverage over other countries: it has a bigger economy and can always threaten withdrawal from the organization. Supporters say free trade will cut prices, increase product quality, and increase revenues by expanding exports and competition. Moreover, because the cost of labor is not the only consideration in producing a good—the education level of labor, technology available, and distribution and transportation systems are other considerations—there will not be a "giant sucking sound" south of the U.S. border. On the contrary, they claim free trade actually creates jobs, particularly export-related jobs, which pay more. Free trade also creates jobs in other countries, which will decrease the flow of illegal immigration from Mexico, Central America, and other economically disadvantaged regions. Finally, proponents of free trade say if the United States does not join in regional and international trade agreements it will be left behind the rest of the world.

So Americans send mixed signals about free trade because they have mixed feelings about free trade. And as long as U.S. politicians rely on the American public to remain in office, they will listen to their constituents and often vote according to the dominant sentiment in their voting districts.

Related information: questions 40, 41

43 : *Isn't America hypocritical when it pushes for access to foreign markets while restraining access to its own?*

One could say that, yes, America is hypocritical when it pushes for access to foreign markets while limiting access to its own, but there are two qualifications to this answer. First, to an extent, *every* country keeps protectionist measures in place it. When it comes to trade, all countries tend to look out for their own interests. However, as trade becomes more global and competitive, there is less tolerance for trade "bullies" and more calls for negotiations.

Second, when the United States threatens to restrain access to its markets, it may be doing just that—*threatening*. A strategy is often involved in such threats; the United States may threaten trade restrictions or sanctions, to urge cooperation in trade disputes, while hoping never to use them. A few examples occurred in 1995.

The Chinese government was not doing what the U.S. government considered an adequate job policing the illegal reproduction and sale of

U.S. compact disks, software, books, licensed trademarks, and other properties. Therefore, to motivate the Chinese government to take action against the "piracy" of such goods, the U.S. government threatened to place 100 percent tariffs on more than one billion dollars' worth of Chinese exports to the United States. The Chinese government eventually promised greater regulation. The threat of sanctions worked, which prompted the U.S. government to try a similar strategy with Japan.

Japanese auto imports were responsible for much of the record U.S. trade deficit with Japan in the early 1990s. Meanwhile, Japan consistently maintained a protective stance relating to its domestic automobile market—a stance that increased tensions between the United States and Japan. Under pressure, Japan agreed in the late 1980s and early 1990s to reduce its auto exports to the United States. But the fact that Japan's domestic market still remained protected angered the U.S. auto industry and government. President Bill Clinton finally indicated that, if Japan did not agree to open its market, the United States would impose sanctions on Japanese automobiles similar to those it threatened to impose on Chinese goods. The Japanese called these threats bullying tactics. However, U.S. and Japanese negotiators reached an agreement just hours before the set deadline. Japan avoided sanctions, and the United States received assurances that Japan's market would accommodate more U.S. autos and auto parts.

Both of these examples illustrate how threatened sanctions helped the United States negotiate relatively rapid, amenable agreements. Again, the United States rarely wants to put threatened protectionist measures in place. Still, when such threats do not lead to agreements, the United States may have to use sanctions to make its threats credible.

Related information: question 39

44 :
Your capitalist system seems to breed an immoral, cutthroat kind of atmosphere. Why are you so against socialism? Isn't it much more humane than capitalism?

The best principles of any political-economic system—be it based on socialism, pluralistic democracy, capitalism, or communism—are humane. They all advocate ideal societies in theory. The question is, how is each system implemented? In a humanitarian sense, "good" and "bad" systems of all types have been implemented throughout history. Therefore, talking about social systems in general terms is somewhat dangerous.

Perhaps many Americans tend to view socialism negatively because they associate a socialist system with communism, particularly Soviet communism. To them, *communism* connotes loss of individual freedom, increase in government control and bureaucracy, atheism, totalitarianism, and eventual economic demise—in short, dictatorial socialism, not democratic socialism.

Most Americans believe a wholly government-planned economy diminishes incentives for innovation, hard work, and individual expression. They distrust government to do for them what they feel they can do better for themselves. They believe society, in general, will run better if capitalist competition prompts people to increase the quality of products and service and decrease costs. However, there are trade-offs in any system, and capitalism is no exception.

The U.S. capitalist system does not reward individuals equally and offers few guarantees to workers about maintaining a given lifestyle. Even so, Americans feel that without inequities there would be no incentives for growth and efficiency. Clearly, in other people's eyes the U.S. capitalist system can involve immoral, cutthroat attitudes and actions, but most Americans believe the benefits of their system outweigh the evils.

Socialism may very well be the best system for a country, depending on the political and social context. Socialism could be ideal when people are trained, conscientious, dedicated, and can make the system work. Americans just haven't adopted it wholeheartedly as a system for them.

However, the U.S. government has assumed some characteristics of social planning at both the state and national levels. In a technical sense, U.S. public schools, police and other emergency forces, and highways and infrastructure projects are publicly funded and, thus, are "social-ized." Hospitals are also socialized in the sense that the paying public subsidizes services for the nonpaying public. Other government-run, tax-supported social programs include Social Security, which supple-ments retiree pensions; Medicare, which provides medical insurance for the elderly; Medicaid, which provides medical insurance for the poor; and additional social welfare programs that give aid to the poor, un-employed, and disabled. In fact, some see the United States as a democratic socialist state because of its substantial mix of private and public sectors.

Speaking in general terms, we all want the most humane, efficient, and productive system for our country. The majority of Americans have concluded that a mixed economy, with both private and public sectors, is the most beneficial. For another people, the best system might be something very different.

Related information: question 31

45 : *If capitalism and democracy are so good for economic growth, why aren't they working in the former Soviet Union and eastern-bloc countries?*

In the past, Western experts generally agreed there was one path to eco-nomic growth and every nation should follow that path, but criticism of this theory has grown over the last several decades. Today, many theo-rists say nations will follow different paths to economic growth because they have different histories and cultures. Those that have a long history of colonization or were under communist rule will develop differently than did the United States or Britain.

These conflicting theories have generated controversy as Russia and other former communist countries attempt to adopt capitalism and democracy and adapt these systems to their present circumstances. Western-based aid institutions, such as the International Monetary Fund (IMF), and Western governments are pressing Russia and other former communist countries to adopt *their* version of capitalism and democracy—to follow what they perceive to be the best path to economic growth. However, leaders of former communist countries claim their circumstances do not allow them to make the transition to democracy and capitalism quickly or in a mandated manner. They say they must be given an opportunity to implement reforms in a manner befitting their histories and present situation.

For example, Russian leaders have argued that they must retain more public economic institutions than are found in Western capitalist countries. And Russian President Boris Yeltsin used force, which many considered undemocratic at best and dictatorial at worst, to keep Chechnya from seceding from Russia in the mid-1990s. He claimed force was necessary to keep Russia united during its formative years as a democracy.[8] It will be interesting to see whose versions of capitalism and democracy—if any—work best in these former communist countries.

Besides conflicting theories and strategies, a number of other obstacles stand in the way of reform and economic growth in former communist countries. Perhaps most importantly, these countries do not enjoy a tradition of open markets. It may take decades to construct basic market institutions, including well-functioning commercial banks, regulatory laws and agencies, a stock exchange, and more. The leaders of these countries have never lived under—let alone governed—a democratic state or a capitalist economic system. They are also attempting to create nation-states out of what was a multiethnic, multinational federa-

---

8. Interestingly, some believe Yeltsin's arguments sounded similar to U.S. President Abraham Lincoln's, who advocated using force to stop the southern states from seceding from the U.S. "Union" in the mid-nineteenth century.

tion. The people are accustomed to the state providing jobs, housing, and other basic necessities. And as freedoms grow so do criminal influences and organized crime; at the same time, laws and the institutions created for their enforcement are new and evolving. All of these changes have brought a sense of instability with them—political and economic instability on a general level and psychological instability on an individual level.

Maintaining patience in overcoming these obstacles will be difficult when inflation is high, jobs are few, food is scarce, and wages are low. In former communist-bloc countries, a vocal faction has promoted a return to nationalism, communism, and authoritarianism. Such calls to turn away from uncertainty and return to familiarity may be attractive to the people suffering under reforms, but they are premature. Making the transition from state-run economies to privatized economies is an unprecedented and monumental task that may take decades to accomplish. Indeed, it is still too early to determine what is or is not working in the countries that once made up the communist bloc. The Polish experiment, however painful it has been, seems to be resulting in economic growth. Hopefully, citizens of other former communist countries will demonstrate the patience needed to allow reforms to bring about a productive transition.

Related information: questions 46, 48, 54

46 : *Why doesn't the United States do more to support economic development in Third World countries? in Russia, the former Soviet Republics, and former eastern-bloc countries?*

Since the end of the Cold War, demands for U.S. aid—from all sides—have only increased. Russia, the other former Soviet republics, and eastern European countries are asking for assistance in developing their economies. Third World countries' demands for economic assistance have grown steadily since the end of World War II. Furthermore, demands from Americans themselves have increased. As the threat of communism—and, therefore, the perceived need to "buy the friendship" of other nations—has diminished, Americans are calling for the U.S. government to make economic development at home a top priority. In short, the United States and its limited capacity to extend aid are stretched very thin.

Even so, the United States continues to support economic development around the world. The U.S. government helps people worldwide by facilitating or providing billions of dollars in agricultural credits and food donations, educational and training programs, medical supplies and treatment, technical and business consultation services, technology transfers, information services, medical and technical research, and more. The government offers this aid autonomously, as well as in conjunction with governments, United Nations agencies, the World Bank, and other organizations. In addition, more U.S. nongovernmental organizations (NGOs) are involved in international development than ever before. U.S. churches, literacy organizations, universities, and other groups sponsor a variety of international grassroots projects aimed at economic and community development. U.S. businesses and private research institutes have entered into a variety of joint ventures to stimulate commerce and benefit the public welfare, particularly in the former Soviet republics.

Yet bringing developing nations into economic parity with countries that have had three centuries of industrial experience remains elusive. Former Soviet republics and other ex-communist countries are rebuilding their economies from the ground up. In the Third World, the standard of living has risen in the past thirty years, and countries have experienced, in some areas, a closing of the economic gap between themselves and industrialized countries, but the gap still exists.

Admittedly, the United States could do more to help. While the United States ranks among the top aid-giving nations, much of the aid the government distributes is never seen by average citizens of recipient countries. Instead it helps countries service their debts or fund their military. U.S. aid is also often distributed based on political or strategic expediency rather than on need. Thus Egypt and Israel, for example, receive far more aid than poorer countries. Plus, in terms of its gross national product and population, the United States falls behind other nations in amount of aid given. Therefore, the United States could sponsor more programs that offer aid directly to those who need it most and could give more aid in terms of per capita expenditures.

The United States could also expand its efforts to help developing nations obtain the technology needed to better compete in the world economy. Because these nations have difficulties gaining capital to invest in technology, U.S. companies could participate in more sharing of up-to-date technologies and joint ventures. The United States will continue to negotiate free-trade agreements worldwide, but it could also help countries work out loan-payment plans that allow them to invest export earnings in economic development rather than in payments. The U.S. government could lessen restrictions on its markets for producers from these countries. Finally, the United States could encourage more foreign investment by U.S. companies that benefits both the companies and the countries involved. Many believe such efforts are more effective than simply giving large sums of money, which are often funneled into and help perpetuate the "old systems" and bureaucracies.

These suggestions are not new. U.S. businesses and government agencies are already involved in promoting these types of ventures. In fact, with increasing demand for the government to address economic problems in America, one of the most promising developments in foreign aid may be the growing number of U.S.-based NGOs. Some even say NGOs working on a grassroots level have a better record of promoting effective economic development than do large-scale government, United Nations, World Bank, or other programs.

Related information: questions 45, 54

47 : *Why don't U.S. development and aid programs, such as those in Latin America and Africa, seem to work?*

In the 1950s and 1960s the goal of development and aid enterprises was "modernization." Development experts, most of whom were economists, believed a country wishing to modernize had to increase its gross national product (GNP) and become more like a Western industrialized democracy. This view of development as economic growth on a large scale and as uniform for all countries influenced thousands of development and aid programs.

During those decades, as well as today, the United States sponsored development and aid projects through large institutions such as the United States Agency for International Development (USAID), the International Monetary Fund (IMF), and the World Bank. The staffs of these institutions consisted predominantly of U.S. economists and engineers who favored modernization in the form of large-scale projects: highways, expensive hydraulic systems, dams, etc. In conjunction with government officials in recipient countries, they designed such projects to be noticed and to make money for investors—not necessarily to be sustainable or environmentally friendly. Development experts lacked extensive knowledge of or contact with the environment, culture, or citizens of recipient countries and often obtained their information from out-of-touch politicians in those countries. In short, projects and programs were "top-down," planned by business representatives and bureaucrats. They did not adequately consider local needs, wants, or resources.

Because planners ignored these important factors for several decades, many development and aid programs were nonproductive at best and harmful at worst. In some cases, aid created a dependency relationship. The United States has sent specialists and supervisors to other countries and has charged substantial fees for their services. These and other practices cause aid recipients to pile up large debts—with interest—for goods or services that are not necessarily wanted or helpful. Money then leaves the country in debt payments rather than being reinvested in native enterprises.

The United States is often blamed for development failures because it is a major investor in the World Bank and other institutions and, thus, influences institutional decisions. But also to blame are officials in recipient countries who agree to unwise projects, accept bribes, or make poor money-management decisions that inhibit their governments from paying back loans. Tighter regulations within countries would help reduce abuse and corruption.

Over the last few decades, the World Bank and other institutions have been rethinking their approach to aid and development. Experts now concede that increasing a country's GNP or sponsoring large-scale projects does not automatically lead to development or help the poor meet their basic needs. More development money is funding basic-needs programs in education, agriculture, health care, and nutrition.

The World Bank has developed a Program of Targeted Interventions, which targets the poorest populations. The U.S. Congress passed the Foreign Assistance Act (1973), which legally binds USAID to provide economic aid to the poorest people in the least developed nations. Other U.S. laws prohibit corporations from bribing foreign government officials to obtain contracts. These laws have not been implemented effectively 100 percent, but they do reflect a new outlook on development and aid. In addition, attempts have been made to make aid programs more accountable for moneys spent and outcomes achieved. And rather than mandate economic reforms, the World Bank and IMF have asked some countries to formulate their own economic plans.

In the 1990s, a new word has become linked with development: *sustainable* development. Large-scale, technically complicated projects still receive funding, but projects that are easy on the environment and can be maintained by natives receive increasing support. The growing number of U.S.-based nongovernmental organizations has also helped focus efforts and attention on grassroots development efforts, such as micro-enterprises, rather than on top-down projects.

Outside aid will always be limited in what it can accomplish. Certainly U.S.-sponsored aid has hurt in some cases more than helped, but though abuses have occurred, most projects are undertaken with honest intent. Individuals and institutions involved in development have learned much over the last several decades about its limitations and problems. Hopefully the knowledge they have gained will shape policies that help the United States use its considerable resources more efficiently, effectively, and sustainably.

Related information: question 48

48 : *Does your government think it can buy our friendship and make us "toe the line" with assistance programs?*

Many, but not all, assistance programs come with restrictions and other "strings" attached.

The United States is an influential member of the International Monetary Fund (IMF), the World Bank, and other institutions that lend money. These institutions often stipulate how loan money should be used and claim the right to impose economic reforms in debtor countries that cannot pay back their loans. They say they must do this to ensure payment and protect the interests of investors and taxpayers from contributing countries.

In the early 1990s, IMF policies toward Russia were particularly controversial. Along with lending Russia money to develop a market economy, the IMF pushed Russia to privatize enterprises and move toward democracy and a capitalist economy. Russia protested that the IMF was pushing change too quickly and that implementing IMF policies would mean inflation, economic depression, and increased hardship for the poor.

Similar situations have resulted in tensions between Third World debtor nations and lending nations, including the United States, Japan, Germany, France, and England. Because the United States is a major contributor to lending institutions, it is often the most harshly criticized for lending policies. Some debtor nations perceive these policies as attempts to inhibit their sovereignty, damage their economies, or otherwise oppress them. They believe lender nations can afford some losses and should offer lower-interest or no-interest loans.

Both sides have a point. Debtor nations could do more to enter into agreements wisely and realistically to ensure they can comply with loan requirements. On the other hand, lender nations could give debtor nations more autonomy and help them devise payment plans that will not adversely affect their poor. There have been recent signs of compromise. In the 1980s and 1990s, the United States negotiated with several less-developed countries to reach debt-handling agreements; these agreements involved forgiving some debts and reducing interest rates.

Another issue might underlie this question: most nations, including the United States, prefer to give aid to allies and/or nations they can influence politically, not necessarily to the most needy countries. During the Cold War—when both sides were vying for support—U.S. aid programs were particularly aimed at gaining friendship and cooperation. Americans thought aid recipients should be grateful and had an obligation to be loyal.

That attitude has diminished slightly since the end of Cold War but not entirely. Still, the United States is learning that money does not buy as much loyalty as it may have in the past. For example, the U.S. government was sending aid to Iraq shortly before Iraq provoked the Persian Gulf War. And although the United States has given billions of dollars to Russia in private and public aid, that country has refused, on several occasions, to bend to U.S. wishes in following its foreign and domestic policies.

But, yes: the United States still extends aid in attempts to extend its influence. All nations do. Aid tying—offering aid on condition of cooperation in military, foreign policy, trade, or other matters—is common. And the fact that the majority of these economic and political relationships continues for decades indicates they are, at least in some ways, mutually beneficial.

It should be mentioned, too, that gaining political advantage is not the primary purpose of all U.S. aid programs. In the 1990s, the United

States extended assistance in Somalia and Haiti primarily for humanitarian purposes. The Peace Corps and numerous aid programs developed by U.S.-based private organizations are also largely meant to aid the needy in less-developed countries and to create goodwill between the United States and other nations.

Related information: questions 45, 47, 56

49 : *It seems as though your businesspeople get rich by exploiting our natural resources and then selling overpriced American goods to us. Is this true?*

It is a common belief that the United States and other industrialized countries take advantage of developing countries by exploiting their natural and financial resources. Exploitation has occurred in the past and, unfortunately, continues today, but probably to a lesser extent. Some early American businesspeople were involved in activities for which there was little precedent. By today's standards they did exploit, but they were not operating in a time of international standards and controls. In fact, some were even encouraged in their exploitative practices by businesspeople and other members of the "elite" in other countries. Hopefully, not all Americans are judged on the actions of unethical opportunists, past or present.

Ideally, governments should protect the interests of their people and check exploitation by ensuring that all businesspeople—foreign and national—obey the law of the land. Proper regulation by the home country of a business as well as by the host country should be a high priority.

Generally speaking, the U.S. government and foreign governments are monitoring business dealings more closely than they have in the past. Nongovernmental organizations and the media have brought examples of exploitative business practices to the public's attention. Publicity about exploitation has prompted "Save the Rain Forest" and other environmental and humanitarian movements. These movements, in turn, have generated demand for tough laws and enforcement. Hopefully this trend will continue.

As for overpriced goods, if your country has a free-market system, then U.S. businesses are free to charge what they will for products. Such practices may not seem fair, particularly if the resources used in producing their products are drawn from your country. But if U.S. companies are overpricing their goods, then the market will likely not sustain them, particularly given the increasingly competitive nature of the world market.

One final note: not all American entrepreneurs "get rich" doing business in and with other countries. Many make risky investments and lose more than they gain. American business often appears to have huge returns on investments because people simply do not notice the cases where U.S. business returns are zero or negative.

50.

The decisions of multinational corporations affect the lives of millions, but their operations and management are a mystery. Who really runs these enormous operations? How are they held accountable? Are multinationals simply fronting for U.S. interests?

Multinational corporations (MNCs) are largely run by managers who are pressured to produce profits by board members, stockholders, and others with money-making interests. Most MNCs are based in Western, industrialized countries, though more are emerging in Asia.

MNCs are regarded as somewhat "lawless" because managers and other employees are not legally liable for decisions made by the corporation as an entity. In addition, they are financially powerful and, thus, can control large chunks of a country's economy. Moreover, many fear that, because MNCs have few ties—cultural, emotional, political, or otherwise—to their host countries, they are liable to exploit those countries' natural and human resources. In short, MNCs are generally regarded as businesses that are not accountable to anyone; they have come to symbolize business "without a human face."

Some say MNCs are not necessarily renegade businesses that feel no sense of responsibility to their host countries. They claim that when a company invests in a country, it becomes bound to that country's economy and will work to ensure the economy remains strong. Some experts argue that transnational investment actually increases economic as well as political cooperation between countries.

But the image of the unaccountable MNC persists. Even the United States has expressed some fears as Japanese and European MNCs invest heavily in U.S. property and business. Strict enforcement of laws in the United States means most of these fears do not materialize. However, countries whose bureaucracies do not or cannot force compliance to laws, tax payments, and responsible operations have experienced great abuses when MNCs have employed bribes to get contracts and financial power and have taken advantage of individuals and governments.

Since the 1960s, when MNCs began to grow and prosper, the press has publicized many such scandals. A U.S.-based MNC reportedly manipulated politics and tried to stop Salvador Allende's 1970 election as president of Chile. In the 1970s, several MNCs were found to have bribed foreign political officials. In 1984, an accident at an MNC-run chemical plant in Bhopal, India, killed more than four thousand people. And in 1981, the marketing practices of a large European corporation that produced baby formula were roundly condemned for putting the health of children in Third World countries at risk.

Increased regulation and enforcement have helped lessen the number of abuses since the 1960s and 1970s, when MNCs were perceived as running wild. International groups such as the World Health Organization and the United Nations have formulated guidelines for MNC products and practices. Other nongovernmental groups and the investigative world press are monitoring MNC activities to a greater extent. The increased publicity surrounding MNCs has prompted public outcry and pressure to right abuses. As a result, laws worldwide are stricter and more widely enforced than before.

Even with increased government crackdowns, some still believe U.S.-based MNCs and the U.S. government are in collusion. They fear MNCs dictate and help carry out U.S. foreign policy or vice versa—that the U.S. government actually runs MNCs. These assertions are not true. There is a real division of power between the U.S. private and public sectors. In many cases, the interests of an MNC and the government are at odds. The U.S. government has objected on several occasions when U.S. companies participated in overseas ventures the government did not regard as proper. And the U.S. government has helped monitor MNC activities at home and abroad. In fact, American businesses sometimes suffer in competition with European and Asian corporations, which enjoy greater protection and support from their home governments. For the most part, however, the extent to which governments can intervene in the interests of MNCs is limited by international agreements.

Related information: question 59

51 : *Isn't your country's use of energy selfish and irresponsible?*
If world supplies of oil and other resources fall short,
those of us in smaller countries will suffer.

Without a doubt, Americans appear to use energy and other resources as if they were inexhaustible. In general, Americans as a people are guilty as charged: because energy is accessible and relatively cheap, they use much more than their fair share. The seven wealthiest countries in the world, including the United States, make up slightly more than 10 percent of the world's population and yet consume nearly 50 percent of some raw materials and forms of energy, as well as produce more than 50 percent of some pollutants.[9]

---

9. Rourke, *International Politics*, 552.

Studies show that the lifestyle most Americans are accustomed to could not be lived by the entire world population. The environment simply would not sustain our consumption-oriented lifestyle on a wide scale.[10] Obviously, because world resources are limited, the Western industrialized nations, particularly the United States, need to rethink their patterns of consumption.

During the energy crises of the 1970s and 1980s, there was evidence that Americans changed some of those patterns. Words such as *insulation, solar power, compact cars,* and *carpooling* all became commonplace. However, since the crises seemingly dissipated, so did the concern and conservative habits of many Americans. Some even believe that the victory of the United States and its allies in the Persian Gulf conflict may have sent the message that the United States can get all the oil it needs.

Actually, most Americans support energy and resource conservation—in theory. But very few are willing to contribute to the cause by making significant changes in their convenient, consumptive lifestyle. Environmentalism has become an increasingly "hot" topic. Perhaps as Americans begin to actually suffer the consequences of their consumption—ozone depletion, toxic beaches, or fuel shortages, for example— they will begin to change their habits, but change takes decades, perhaps even generations.

The 1992 United Nations Conference on Environment and Development in Rio de Janeiro showed that Third World countries are asserting their right to develop and holding Northern nations accountable for their consumption and pollution. It will be interesting to see, over the next several decades, how industrialized nations and their citizens respond to the prospect of sharing a shrinking resource base with a growing, developing, and increasingly powerful and politically active Third World.

Related information: questions 18, 63, 70

---

10. Alan During, "How Much Is 'Enough?'" *World•Watch* 3, no. 6 (November/ December 1990): 14.

CHAPTER FOUR

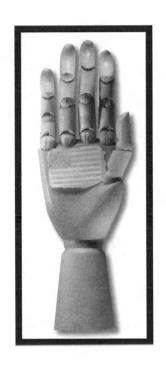

FOUR

AMERICAN
FOREIGN
POLICY

Since 1989, the world has been transformed. For one-half century, from the end of World War II (1945), the single overriding consideration of American foreign policy was the Soviet Union. The principal focus of American policy was containing communism. Most international conflicts, no matter how remote or local in origin—from Vietnam to Angola to Nicaragua—quickly became confrontations between the United States and the USSR.[1]

Then suddenly, unexpectedly, the Cold War was over. The confrontation between the United States and the Soviet Union came to an abrupt

---

1. The exact time frame for U.S. involvement in these conflicts is difficult to determine. Support for the South Vietnamese government stretched over decades, but open U.S. military support is generally accepted as beginning in 1964 with the Tonkin Gulf Resolution. The United States pulled out of Vietnam in 1975. U.S. involvement in the Angolan independence movement began in the 1960s, and while the Angolan civil war is no longer an East-West conflict, the United States continues to encourage reconciliation in that African country. American interests and intervention in Nicaragua date back to the 1800s. During the Cold War, Nicaragua became a hot spot when Daniel Ortega's Sandinistas came to power (1979) and developed relations with the Soviet Union. The United States not only supported the Sandinistas' rivals, the contras, with arms and intelligence but mined Nicaragua's harbors (1983–84). U.S. leverage apparently paid off when Violeta Chamorro was elected as Nicaragua's president (1990), and more favorable relations with the United States resulted.

end. It was not anticipated, but it happened—much faster than anyone expected. In 1989, the Berlin Wall collapsed, East Germany disintegrated, and Germany, which had been divided for more than four decades, was suddenly a single nation once again. Within a few months of the dismantling of the Berlin Wall, the Soviet Union ceased to exist. Instead of a superpower, there were fifteen individual republics with disintegrating economies, internal ethnic conflicts, and populations facing an uncertain future.

The foreign policy challenges facing the United States in this changed world have been completely altered as well. Americans are witnessing the difficult struggle to establish democratic political systems, pluralistic societies, and market-oriented economies in the republics that were formerly constituent parts of the Soviet Union. The former Soviet satellites in central and eastern Europe are eagerly pressing for membership in the European Union and seeking full participation in the North Atlantic Treaty Organization (NATO). Assuring the democratization of these former communist countries is a critical and urgent task facing the United States and the world. While China remains a communist state, market-oriented economic development there is forcing profound economic, social, and political changes that have international ramifications. Population growth and economic stagnation in a number of developing countries are creating serious difficulties for these countries, but the consequences of their problems may well spill beyond their borders to create broader international difficulties.

Thus, while the conclusion of the Cold War has brought an end to the superpower confrontation, it has not brought stability or tranquillity. For the United States, it has brought unprecedented challenges. The principles that guided American foreign policy from the end of World War II are no longer valid in the post-Cold War world. America now confronts serious—but new, very different, and much less-focused—threats to its security and national interests.

One of the most serious and dangerous problems the international community is facing is the proliferation of nuclear arms, chemical and biological weapons, and their delivery systems. As America's experience with Iraq during the Persian Gulf War (1990–91) demonstrated, less-developed countries can acquire nuclear arms and other highly destructive weapons if they have the will to do so. This has been confirmed by North Korea, which has undertaken a serious effort to develop nuclear weapons. There are clear indications that Iran, too, is pursuing policies to develop nuclear weapons capabilities. Meanwhile, China has sold sophisticated missiles to Pakistan, which give Pakistan the ability to deliver the nuclear weapons it has already acquired. The continuing confrontation over Kashmir between Pakistan and India, another country with nuclear weapons, raises serious questions for the world community. The collapse of the Soviet Union has led to a significant reduction in the risk of a massive nuclear confrontation involving the United States. Even so, the world faces a significantly increased risk that nuclear materials from missiles in former Soviet republics—Russia, Ukraine, Belarus, and Kazakhstan—might be acquired by terrorists. Thus far, fortunately, only small quantities of weapons-grade nuclear material and larger amounts of non-weapons-grade material have fallen into criminal hands, and international cooperation in dealing with illicit trade of nuclear materials has been excellent, but the threat of "loose nukes" is very serious and very real.

Matters that in the past were "domestic" are increasingly becoming international issues. Ethnic conflict and broad concern for the observance of human rights raises questions about the balance between national sovereignty and threats to the stability of the international community. Collective security may require the coordination of international intervention to stop or prevent human-rights violations and destabilizing interethnic or interreligious conflicts. Indeed, the international community faces increased levels of interethnic strife; the tragic and bloody violence that has gripped Bosnia and other republics of the former Yugoslavia is only one of the most tragic examples. The world faces similar potential problems in many areas of the former Soviet Union: the conflict between Armenia and Azerbaijan and the ethnic conflicts in Georgia and Chechnya are but three examples. Communal violence in India between Hindus and Muslims continues to fester and periodically erupts with great violence. Comparable problems are waiting to explode in many other places around the globe.

Another issue that is often considered a "domestic" problem, but in fact is a serious international issue, is migration. Even established democracies like the United States, Germany, and the democratic states of western Europe are having difficulty adjusting to the massive influx of refugees and immigrants that is straining the social fabric and testing the limits of tolerance of diversity. The substantial pressures for migration to the United States from Mexico, Central America, Cuba, and Haiti have had significant effects on U.S. foreign policy.

Terrorism continues, but with new and more frightening manifestations, and without some of the restraints the Cold War imposed in the past. Some countries are involved in state-sponsored terrorism clandestinely; with government knowledge and support, terrorist groups are engaged in an effort to undermine and destroy the status quo. A number of countries have been identified as officially supporting terrorism, including Iraq, Iran, North Korea, Libya, Syria, and Cuba. In addition, the world faces increased violence through substate terrorism from groups such as Islamic radicals in Algeria, Egypt, and other Muslim countries. The New York World Trade Center bombing in 1993 raised troubling questions about the spread of such international terrorist threats to the United States.

In Rwanda, Somalia, and other countries we have seen the tragedy of failed societies—countries where the political and economic communities have disintegrated and the fabric of civilization has unraveled, resulting in human suffering, chaos, and brutality. Failed societies represent a serious post-Cold War challenge to U.S. national interests and a humanitarian concern for the United States and the world community.

The United States and the world community face unparalleled challenges in this new international environment. They must establish new structures and principles to guide states' actions in the international arena.

It is clear that collective security must be defined more inclusively because of our international interdependence, worldwide telecommunications, and global financial and economic markets. It is also clear that collective security includes what now fashionably are called "transnational issues": support for and encouragement of democracy; the fight against international terrorism, the narcotics trade, and other forms of crime; protection of the global environment; world population control; arms control; and prevention of nuclear, chemical, or biological weapons proliferation.

As the world community faces the insecurity and uncertainty of the post-Cold War world, the United Nations has been seen by some as an instrument through which America can accomplish its foreign policy objectives. The disintegration of the Soviet Union and the end of the Soviet-American conflict have enhanced the ability of the United Nations (UN) Security Council to take cooperative action in dealing with threats to global security. The international effort in the Persian Gulf War is perhaps the best example of how fundamentally things have changed. At the same time, the inability of the United Nations to bring an end to the long-festering conflict in Bosnia raises doubts about just how much the United Nations can accomplish without decisive American leadership. The Bush administration's decisive handling of the Iraqi occupation of Kuwait (1990–91) starkly contrasts with its failure to act in the crisis in the former Yugoslavia, which began at the same time. It seems clear that strong American leadership is critical for UN success.

The international community must seriously consider the extent to which the United Nations is capable of handling an expanded role in international security. Some doubt the congruity of interests among key member states and groups of states that would permit decisive action. Other fundamental questions concern the United Nations's ability to manage the complexities of peacekeeping responsibilities that have increasingly fallen upon the organization.

Members of Congress and Americans in general have increasingly debated the role that the United States should play in the United

Nations and in international peacekeeping activities. A strong and vocal element opposes U.S. participation in the United Nations in any form—but particularly in activities that involve foreign command of American forces—fearing a loss of U.S. sovereignty. Others argue that active involvement in the United Nations gives the United States an additional means to further its foreign policy interests by involving other countries in common pursuits. The United States must resolve the questions regarding what role collective action under UN auspices—and U.S. participation in peacekeeping, peace-enforcing, and peacemaking actions—will play in formulating foreign policy.

A critical related question, which has become highly relevant in the changed international terrain after the Cold War, is the role of the North Atlantic alliance. The North Atlantic Treaty and NATO, the organizational structure for implementing the treaty, was established in 1949 specifically to deal with the threat to Western Europe of an aggressive, expansionist Soviet Union. Now that the Soviet Union no longer exists and Western Europe has established new economic and political bonds in the European Union, the United States must rethink and reevaluate the role of NATO. While the North Atlantic alliance continues to reflect the interests of a broad community—the United States, Canada, and western Europe—questions have been raised about the role of NATO in a world without a Soviet Union, since the very reason for its existence and its structure was to meet the challenge of the Soviet Union. Various proposals have been advanced regarding the future of NATO and the potential roles for NATO in UN peacekeeping activities. The vigorous NATO action in bombing Bosnian Serb military targets in the fall of 1995 showed the organization's military strength, but the key element is political agreement among NATO members about what action is appropriate for the alliance under these changed international conditions.

NATO has made the decision to expand its membership to include eventually some or all of the former communist nations of central and eastern Europe and even republics of the former Soviet Union. The NATO Partners for Peace Initiative (1994) is designed to increase affiliation during this period of transition. Nevertheless, there are fundamental questions about the nature and purpose of the alliance under these conditions.

A serious and vigorous public debate continues regarding the objectives and means available to the United States in protecting its national security in the post-Cold War world. A strong isolationist element has emerged in that debate over U.S. international involvement. This isolationism is eerily reminiscent of America in the 1920s and 1930s when America's refusal to become involved in international affairs contributed to the rise of Nazi Germany, fascist Italy, and militaristic Japan. Americans pressing for U.S. withdrawal from international participation reason that, since the West won the Cold War, the United States can now forget the rest of the world and deal with its internal problems. Those who take this position press to maintain a strong military. But they strongly oppose any U.S. military involvement beyond U.S. borders unless vital national security interests are at stake, and their interpretation of vital interests is extremely narrow.

Others argue for American engagement in the world. They point out that the international order of the future is being established and that the United States has a long-term national interest in assuring international order, stability, and respect for fundamental human and civil rights. They argue that the United States has broad economic, political, and cultural links with the rest of the world and, thus, has a serious interest in the international order. They claim Americans have an obligation to ensure a world order that is conducive to the protection and pursuit of U.S. interests.

These dramatic international changes and this American debate form the backdrop to considering questions about and responses to U.S. foreign policy. This is a time when the principles that guide U.S. policy are not as crystal clear as they have been in the past and a time when America is experiencing a vigorous national debate about the appropriate direction of foreign policy in the future. While the continuing debate makes giving definitive responses to foreign visitors more difficult, it also demonstrates the robust health of our democratic society.

We're confused by the direction of U.S. foreign policy since the end of the Cold War. How will the United States operate without anticommunism as its central organizing principle? Is America growing increasingly isolationist? We have relied on you in the past, but now you seem to be more involved with your domestic problems. Is your power shrinking?

52 :

The guiding premise for U.S. foreign policy has not changed since the late nineteenth century (and, some might say, even earlier): spreading democracy and expanding U.S. markets. Some would argue, however, that during the Cold War the focus of U.S. foreign policy was as much anticommunist as it was pro-democracy. Now, free from the threat of communist expansion, the U.S. government shows signs of once again maintaining its primary focus on pro-democracy and pro-free-market activities. For instance, the Clinton administration in 1993 enunciated a policy meant to refocus efforts from containing communism and spreading American interests to simply spreading American interests. The policy sought to enlarge the world's market democracies by (1) strengthening existing market democracies; (2) facilitating the development of new market democracies, particularly in regions of humanitarian concern; and (3) countering hostility aimed at impeding that development.[2]

Clearly, the development of new market economies can only enhance American financial opportunities abroad. The United States's involvement in negotiating the North American Free Trade Agreement, the Uruguay Round of the General Agreement on Trade and Tariffs, and regional trade agreements shows that market economics will continue to play a significant—and even growing—role in post-Cold War foreign policy making.

Is America focusing more on domestic problems? Yes. But that is a fairly typical pattern after war—even a cold war. After maintaining an outward focus for so long, the American public is turning its attention

---

2. Anthony Lake, "From Containment to Enlargement" (address given at the School of Advanced International Studies, Johns Hopkins University, 21 September 1993).

to domestic concerns and would like its government to do the same. In 1992, Americans voted for Bill Clinton over George Bush. Bush's acknowledged strength was foreign policy, but Clinton won votes with his promise to focus more on troubles at home than troubles abroad. Americans today generally support a more domestic-focused agenda, dedicated to the problems of a weak economy, an enormous federal-budget deficit, crime, health care, and unemployment.

Does this mean America is growing increasingly isolationist? No. In fact, it would be difficult to demonstrate that America was ever isolationist. Studies show that Americans believe the United States should remain involved in world affairs, send U.S. troops abroad under certain circumstances, and be an active member of the United Nations. However, the United States lacks the desire and the resources to be the world's *sole* leader or (as some term it) policeman.[3] Instead, it will likely seek to play an active role in the world—*in conjunction with other countries.* The Clinton administration called its policy "assertive multilateralism," meaning that the United States would play a leading role in the United Nations and other organizations that rally the efforts and resources of multiple governments.[4]

Does this indicate America's power is shrinking? Some argue that the United States is now the only superpower. Others say the United States's power stemmed from its strong economy after World War II and its role as the chief opponent of communist doctrine. Thus, its power eroded with the rise of new economic powers and the erosion of communist rule in Europe and the former USSR. Both of these arguments hold a grain a truth. But in the future world, which will likely grow more and more interdependent, the United States's power will probably stem from its ability to gain the cooperation and organize the efforts of many countries.

Related information: questions 53, 54, 57

---

3. Kenneth Jost, "Foreign Policy and Public Opinion: Have Americans Grown Tired of World Affairs?" *CQ Researcher* 4, no. 26 (15 July 1994): 606–7, 610, 615.

4. Mary H. Cooper, "Foreign Policy Burden: Should the U.S. Police the World in the Post-Cold War Era? *CQ Researcher* 3, no. 31 (20 August 1993): 727–28, 733, 737.

53 :
What determines foreign intervention on the part of the United States? Why does your country continue to "police" other nations, especially in light of what happened in Vietnam.

Since World War II, the United States has made mistakes by intervening abroad. In retrospect, we can see that policy makers' thinking was distorted by the context of the Cold War. The Vietnam policy, which was driven by an unfounded fear that communism would take over all of Asia, is just one example. In hindsight, Americans can now see the mistaken assumptions that helped form that policy. The United States went into Vietnam ignorant about the people, interests, needs, and cultures of Southeast Asia; lacking the full support of Americans; overestimating the abilities of U.S. forces; and underestimating the abilities and nationalism of the Vietnamese.

Some say post-Vietnam America has finally recognized the limits of its power. Undoubtedly, Vietnam left Americans hesitant about military intervention abroad. Some in the international community, who believe America oversteps its bounds in "policing" other nations, are happy about that, while others find U.S. reticence frustrating. Most are left uncertain of when the United States will intervene, either militarily, diplomatically through negotiations, or economically through sanctions and embargoes.

It is difficult to outline any hard-and-fast principles of intervention. If a president were to outline a complete checklist of necessary circumstances for U.S. intervention, such a checklist could be misinterpreted by international leaders and restrict the president's flexibility.[5] In addition, every administration will respond somewhat differently to situations abroad. Much depends on the president and his advisors: when some would intervene others might not. Yet several principles of intervention remain fairly constant, most of which involve national interests,

---

5. Madeleine K. Albright, remarks given at the National War College, National Defense University, Fort Lesley J. McNair, Washington, D.C., 23 September 1993.

moral ideals, and/or national stability. Americans generally feel that when these principles are at risk, intervention or "policing" is justified.

National security—the security of both the United States and its people—has always been considered the primary cause for intervention. "National interests" is another cause for intervention and can take a variety of forms. As the global economy plays a greater part in determining foreign policy, economic/trade concerns will almost certainly come increasingly under the heading of "national interests." Before and during the Persian Gulf War, the Bush administration focused on the human-rights violations Iraqis were committing in Kuwait, as well as the political rights of Kuwaitis to be self-determining and stand up to unprovoked aggression. However, most believe the principal reason for U.S. intervention was the potential for the Middle Eastern oil trade to come under Saddam Hussein's control, which would have affected the "national interests" of the United States and many other nations.

Other reasons for intervention include threats against the security of U.S. allies, such as fellow members of the North Atlantic Treaty Organization. Threats to basic human rights usually prompt economic, rather than military, intervention. The United States's withholding of aid and imposing of sanctions in South Africa, in formal protest of its apartheid policies, is one such example. The United States has also intervened for other humanitarian reasons, including famine. Deposed democratic rule and imposed dictatorial rule have evoked U.S. response; in Haiti, U.S. government representatives negotiated with junta leaders, paving the way for Jean-Bertrand Aristide, the democratically elected president, to return (1994).

Other factors come into play as well. Geographic proximity plays a definite role. Had the situation in Haiti presented itself halfway around the globe, the United States would likely not have intervened. Because of geographic considerations, many Americans believed Europeans should have taken the lead in the post-Cold War Bosnian conflict rather than rely on U.S. leadership. Political pressure is another important factor. United Nations Secretary-General Boutros Boutros-Ghali hinted that no one paid attention to Somalia because of racial prejudice; he thereby undoubtedly influenced the U.S. government's decision to intervene there (1992–94). Another factor is the measure of support the United States is promised by others in the international community. The Persian Gulf War was considered successful in large part because President George Bush was able to gain the military and/or financial support of more than thirty countries.

Finally, the American public must be willing to support the cost of intervention, both in economic and human terms. In post-Vietnam America, the public is less willing to commit resources, especially human lives, to military causes abroad. This reticence affects the decisions of policy makers about when to engage *and* disengage U.S. resources. Policy makers are more wary of "mission creep"—of maintaining U.S. forces and resources abroad beyond an established time frame or mission scope. The U.S. interventions in Grenada (1983), Panama (1989–90), the Persian Gulf, and Haiti (1994–95) were the quick-in-and-quick-out variety. They either involved the prompt removal of troops or the turning over of responsibilities to multinational forces. In Somalia, on the other hand, decision makers expanded the mission from lifesaving to nation-building purposes; but when U.S. soldiers were killed, and one was dragged through the streets of Somalia's capital, Americans wanted their troops returned home. In immediately reporting the human costs of military intervention abroad, the U.S. press has undoubtedly affected the government's tendencies to get involved in low-risk, short-term military interventions. The Cable News Network (CNN), which broadcasts world news around the clock and is available practically worldwide, has had a significant impact on public opinion of world events, both within and outside of the United States.

It will be interesting to see how U.S. intervention policy develops in the post-Cold War world. The worldwide trend is definitely toward greater regional, ethnic, religious, and domestic clashes—messy situations in which the United States is hesitant to intervene. Many, at home and abroad, say American has a humanitarian interest to become involved in such clashes. Others believe America has neither the resources nor the right to do so. The debate between interests, rights, and resources will undoubtedly be a heated one in the decades ahead.

Related information: question 52, 60

54 : *With the collapse of the Soviet Union and the alleviation of some of the pressures previously imposed on the United States, what are your country's goals or objectives in relation to that region?*

Russia and other Soviet successor states have had their share of problems accompanying the "opening" of their societies: economic hardship, crime and corruption, a widening gap between rich and poor, pro-communist and extreme nationalist movements, and ethnic tensions. These problems—taken individually or collectively—have the potential to jeopardize the movement toward democracy in the former Soviet republics. But since the fall of communist rule, the United States has shown itself to be committed to helping market democracies develop and diffusing any potential for conflict in the region.

The U.S. government has sponsored rounds of disarmament talks and several disarmament agreements with the Soviet successor states, particularly with those that possess nuclear weapons; in addition, it has provided the region with large sums of money to aid in defense-conversion efforts. Such talks and agreements are not only in the interest of the United States but in the interest of the world. They reduce the chance that nuclear war will break out in the volatile region and effectively halt the progress these new nations are making toward democracy.

The United States has also provided Russia and other former Soviet republics with aid in three general categories. First, the government has donated and distributed humanitarian assistance in the form of food, medicines, and medical supplies and has established joint ventures and exchanges between U.S. and other agencies to study health-care resources and disease in the region. Second, the U.S. government and private American organizations have donated technical assistance—consultation services, exchange programs, research findings, loans, grants, etc.—in the following areas: agriculture and agribusiness, health care, energy production and efficiency, business/privatization, and democratic-institution building, i.e., law, public administration, political processes, and journalism. Third, the U.S. government has provided the region with billions of dollars in credit guarantees to purchase U.S. agricultural products.[6] Again, the United States has given this aid—and has urged other countries to do likewise—to help former communist nations develop their democratic and market institutions and to help quell the resentment that often accompanies, and could potentially disrupt, economic and political reforms.

Although some policies of the new governments in eastern Europe have been so inconsistent and restrictive as to drive private U.S. companies away, the U.S. government continues to promote foreign investment in and trade with the former eastern bloc. In fact, trade is preferred to aid by both sides. Trade mutually benefits each country involved—while aid does not—and aid often comes with conditions that are difficult to meet. If the new governments do not meet these conditions, Western aid may be withdrawn. However, if imposed conditions negatively impact the citizens of these new nations, nationalist and pro-communist feelings tend to grow. So the new leaders of these nations often face a lose-lose dilemma in accepting Western aid. In general, trade does not pose such dilemmas. Promoting joint ventures between U.S. businesses, laboratories, and other institutions in former communist countries is one way the United States has attempted to help the economies and research programs in these countries.

---

6. For more specific information regarding U.S. aid to the region, and particularly to Russia, see periodic reports in the *U.S. Department of State Dispatch*, e.g., "Fact Sheet: U.S. Assistance to Russia," *U.S. Department of State Dispatch Supplement* 4, no. 3 (August 1993): 13–16; "Fact Sheet: Russia," *U.S. Department of State Dispatch* 4, no. 33 (16 August 1993): 579–83.

For the first few years after the fall of communist rule in Europe, U.S. relations with that region were fairly smooth and positive, but relations were tried to a greater extent by the mid-1990s. The Russian and U.S. governments clashed over several issues: the war in the former Yugoslavia, Russia's plans to sell nuclear reactors to Iran, Russia's use of force to squelch the Chechnyan rebellion, and the expansion of NATO to include former eastern-bloc countries. Still, the United States believes the continued development of market democracies is in the best interest of that region, the United States, and the rest of the world. It will continue to foster development as long as the region's governments are amenable to help.

Related information: questions 45, 46, 48, 52

55 : *Is the United States truly attempting to make major cuts in arms expenditures? What are the implications for your military and defense industries?*

With the relaxation and then the end of the Cold War, the United States has cut arms expenditures.[7] The defense budget has been cut—not only because of growing international pressure but because Americans are pressuring the government to devote more resources to domestic issues. U.S. government representatives have reached major arms-reduction agreements—such as Start I and Start II—with Russia and other former Soviet republics and are negotiating agreements with other nations. The U.S. government hopes that, by promoting disarmament at home and abroad, it can stigmatize nuclear and other weapons and promote peace.

Of course, the fact that the U.S. Department of Defense is spending considerably less than it did during the height of the Cold War holds

---

7. The following served as a general source for the information contained in this response: Mary H. Cooper, "Arms Sales: Should the U.S. Cut Its Weapons Exports?" *CQ Researcher* 4, no. 46 (9 December 1994): 1081–1104.

serious implications. Military-base closures mean millions of jobs lost by military and civilian personnel. Private industries involved in manufacturing military equipment must also reduce their workforces by hundreds of thousands of employees. Politicians have discussed the possibility of converting defense industries to produce domestic goods, but little industry conversion has taken place. Instead, industries have slashed their workforces and/or increased exports to remain profitable.

Even in the face of budget cuts, however, the U.S. military has been able to continue improving the technology it uses; many improvements are based on lessons learned during the Persian Gulf War. In addition, tighter budgets force the military to implement some cost-saving procedures, such as recycling and using more cost-effective materials—procedures that some say are long overdue. And it should be pointed out that the U.S. defense budget is still larger than the combined defense budgets of the other NATO members.

Still, military cuts remain controversial. Although the world is safer in terms of the possibility of a nuclear-superpower confrontation, regional and in-country conflicts are expected to increase. Thus, politicians want to maintain a balance between a too-high military budget and a budget that does not adequately provide for the defense of the United States and its allies. Republican politicians are typically less willing to dramatically cut military spending while Democratic politicians are typically willing to cut more. So the level of military spending often depends on who is president and which is the majority party in the House of Representatives and the Senate.

At times it may seem that Americans are against military cuts, but that perception is generally not true. News stories focus on U.S. politicians and citizens protesting the closing of military bases or weapons facilities, but Americans usually oppose military-spending cuts only when cuts lead to lower revenues or fewer jobs for them. Politicians, therefore, will often oppose cuts to facilities in their areas because loss of revenues or jobs for their constituents may mean a loss of votes in the next election.

Related information: question 56

56 : *If America truly wants peace, why do you export so many arms to other nations? Hasn't that practice backfired?*

It seems certain that international arms sales will continue, even in the post-Cold War era.[8] In fact, the end of the Cold War has contributed to sales in a number of ways. Many nations are now less fearful that exported arms might somehow be transferred to communist countries or allies. In addition, because the two superpowers are not vying for friends or lending their forces to proxy wars, smaller nations feel more threatened. They are arming themselves against the growing threat of regional conflicts and small-scale wars. And U.S. manufacturers are willing to supply them with arms. The United States is now the world's largest weapons supplier. Ironically, U.S. arms exports are growing even while American representatives negotiate disarmament agreements around the world.

In the post-Cold War world, where arms reductions at home are the norm, export sales help keep industries going. Due to U.S. military budget cuts, American firms are now looking to overseas markets. Manufacturers receive a number of benefits by increasing their exports. Sales increase; producing more arms keeps the cost per unit produced down; and producing arms for export keeps production lines open so that when new weapons technology is developed it can be produced readily.

Arms manufacturers have political clout and sometimes encourage the government to facilitate export deals for them. Arms workers are also politically powerful and lobby hard to keep their jobs. Politicians often work to keep plants open when industry employees are in their voting district. It is in their interest, as well as the interest of their constituents, to see that local industries have a market, if not domestically then overseas.

Financial benefits and industry stability are not the only reasons the United States exports arms. The United States also exports arms to allies in hopes that recipient countries will show support for the United States

8. The following served as general sources for the information contained in this response: Cooper, "Arms Sales"; John T. Rourke, *International Politics on the World Stage*, 4th ed. (Guilford, Conn.: Dushkin Publishing Group, 1993), 365–71, 418–19.

and its policies. By buying U.S. arms, other nations' militaries become more closely aligned with the U.S. military and more dependent on U.S. supplies. So exporting arms usually gains the United States some political influence.

However, that influence is not long lasting in many cases. In the Persian Gulf War, some of Iraq's weapons came indirectly from the United States, by way of Saudi Arabia. France, Britain, Egypt, Russia, and Kuwait had also sold weapons to Iraq that were used against allied troops in the war. In Panama and Somalia, U.S. troops encountered opposition forces that the United States had helped arm. The weapons U.S. soldiers faced in these conflicts were not always directly traceable to the United States, but U.S. industry and government contributed to the arms buildup in both countries. Weapons provided to such countries may help U.S. industries thrive, but as some critics have pointed out, they cost the United States billions of dollars in the long run. After the Persian Gulf War, the major industrialized nations seemed to have learned a hard lesson: they agreed to limit their arms sales abroad, particularly to the Middle East.

Arms sales can hurt the United States in other ways as well. The governments of developing countries often spend more money on weapons than on meeting the basic needs of their citizens. This practice ends up costing the United States aid dollars. Frequently, arms are given away as a form of foreign aid, which costs U.S. taxpayers as well. It is also difficult for the U.S. government to effectively persuade other nations to limit their arms sales or acquisitions when the United States is responsible for the majority of the world's arms sales. And due to the interdependent nature of the world economy, when other governments invest more in arms than in domestic economic development, the U.S. economy suffers as well. Finally, infinitely more significant than any financial impact is the cost of arms proliferation in terms of loss of human life, on a grand scale, and increased tyranny worldwide. So yes: exporting arms can backfire, in more ways than one.

Related information: questions 48, 55

57
.
:
.
The United States seems to want to let the United Nations (UN) lead when it comes to peacekeeping. Why do you hang back until others have made up their minds?

Actually, in the 1990s, the United States took leading roles in several UN interventions, including those in the Persian Gulf, Somalia, and Haiti. However, it has held back in other situations (Bosnia and Rwanda, for example) where its leadership may have made a difference in UN involvement.

The United States has found itself in a difficult position since the end of the Cold War. It is the only "superpower" that survived intact and, therefore, feels an obligation and some international pressure to take a leadership role. Even most Americans believe the United States should continue to be actively involved in the international community and in the United Nations. On the other hand, the nation's resources are finite, and Americans are calling for more of those resources to be devoted to domestic issues. Plus, they seem increasingly leery of getting involved in messy disputes abroad that could cost American lives. So U.S. policy makers face conflicting sentiments at home and abroad about the role the United States should take in UN peacekeeping missions.

Compounding the problem of these mixed messages is the fact that the presidency changes hands relatively frequently in the United States, and different presidents (who are the nation's chief foreign policy makers) have different opinions of the United Nations. While Ronald Reagan seemed to distrust the United Nations, George Bush worked with it in organizing the Persian Gulf and Somalia missions. Bill Clinton seemed willing to take a leadership role in certain UN missions, though he warned that, to gain U.S. cooperation, "the United Nations must know when to say no."[9]

Indeed, the United States cannot afford to play a leading role in every dispute around the world or in every UN *mission*. But it can—and

---

9. Quoted in Thomas L. Friedman, "Theory vs. Practice," *New York Times*, 1 October 1993, late edition, sec. A.

very likely will—continue to play a leading role in the United Nations *organization* and in other multinational organizations. The Clinton administration's policy, termed "assertive multilateralism," assumed that America would play a leading role within multinational organizations (rather than a lone-superpower role).[10] Assertive multilateralism will likely be a policy of the future for several reasons: U.S. resources are limited, but the United States still feels an obligation to be a leader and does not want its interests overlooked or disregarded.

Related information: question 52

58 : *Will the United States stay engaged in Europe and the North Atlantic Treaty Organization (NATO)?*

There is no doubt that—at least militarily—the United States's presence in NATO has decreased; U.S. troops in Europe have been cut by tens of thousands since the end of the Cold War.[11] Even so, some Americans and Europeans believe the United States still maintains too strong a presence in NATO. France, for example, has long resented the influence the United States tends to wield in NATO and in European affairs in general. Some think Europe no longer needs America's nuclear backing to deter Soviet aggression, particularly given the success of disarmament talks. Some in the United States believe their government should focus on economic rather than military involvement in Europe. While others say the U.S. government should devote more resources to domestic issues now that the Soviet threat has diminished.

In addition, many point to the organizations Europe has maintained on its own that are dedicated to defense and security issues: the Conference on Security and Cooperation in Europe (CSCE); the Western Eu-

---

10. Cooper, "Foreign Policy Burden," 727–28, 733, 737.

11. The following served as a general source for the information contained in this response: Mary H. Cooper, "NATO's Changing Role: Does the Old Atlantic Alliance Have a Post-Cold War Role?" *CQ Researcher* 2, no. 31 (21 August 1992): 713–36.

ropean Union (WEU); and the Franco-German brigade, which some see as the start of a European Community Army that will eventually replace NATO.

Still many, including the majority of U.S. political leaders, argue that the United States has a continued interest and a right to be involved in European security. They point to the democratic traditions that link the United States and Europe as well as the two world wars the United States helped Europe fight. Many believe if the United States is not involved in NATO, it will not feel obligated to defend NATO countries from aggression within Europe (some fear a resurgent Germany) or outside of Europe (some fear a resurgent Russia). Some say Europe cannot afford to let go of the United States's still-substantial military resources. While others believe the United States provides an even more valuable resource—an "outside voice" that often helps negotiate a European consensus.

U.S. leaders have clearly indicated their desire to stay involved in NATO. However, President George Bush, concerned about the strengthening of European-only security organizations, said Europe should "say so" if it wanted to go its "own way." Indeed, if Europe calls more loudly for a greater U.S. military withdrawal, the American public will likely call for the same, and U.S. leaders may oblige.

The United States showed reluctance to take a leadership role in the post-Cold War Bosnian crisis. But the fact that the former Yugoslavia was not a NATO member complicated the situation. Americans felt Europeans should take action because Bosnia-Herzegovina was in their "backyard," and the national interests of European countries were more at stake than those of the United States. But neither Europeans nor Americans wanted to get heavily involved in a messy territorial dispute with ethnic dynamics.

In the future, some key decisions will have to be made by NATO leaders. They will have to decide whether NATO becomes involved in smaller, domestic disputes, such as the war in Bosnia, which many believe will only become more prevalent. They will have to decide whether

NATO will take action outside of pact-members' territory (in areas such as Bosnia) and even outside of Europe (in areas such as the Persian Gulf). They will also have to decide which countries will be offered membership and how membership decisions will affect relations with excluded nations, namely Russia. Not least of the key decisions facing NATO concerns the future involvement of the United States.

59

Who makes foreign policy in the United States? Presidents in the past have reached agreements only to have your congress reverse them. We're confused. Don't big business and multinational corporations based in the United States determine U.S. foreign policy to a great extent?

In general terms, the responsibility for U.S. foreign policy lies with the president and his officers in the executive branch. Constitutionally, however, the Congress has an important role to play, and since support money is generally provided by Congress, Congress finds ways to limit the president's powers.

According to the Constitution, presidential *treaties* are subject to the advice and consent of the Senate; they must receive a two-thirds vote in the U.S. Senate or they are not approved. However, many presidents have claimed that, as commanders in chief, they have the power to make executive *agreements* with other governments, without the Senate's consent. Even government officials are not always sure where the line between treaty and agreement lies. In some cases, presidents have been accused of resorting to agreements when they knew a treaty would not pass the Senate.

If the executive branch takes a heavy-handed approach to foreign policy, Congress can try to reverse presidential agreements or curtail the president's powers in another way. During the unpopular Vietnam War, for example, Congress tempered the president's powers to commit U.S. troops to foreign conflicts by passing the War Powers Resolution.

Many other groups and individuals can affect foreign policy. Certainly public opinion is an important factor. Because politicians depend on voters for their jobs, opposition from or support by the American public can determine whether politicians oppose or support a given policy. Public opinion, in turn, is affected by the media. Many believe the United States would not have intervened in Somalia had the American public not been moved by pictures of starving people. Ironically, the pictures of U.S. soldiers being captured and killed led the American public to demand the withdrawal of U.S. troops from Somalia.[12] Even so, decision makers must strike a balance between relying too much and too little on public opinion. The American people want to be heard, but they do not want a president who fails to take a stand—however unpopular—or who delays every decision while waiting for public-opinion poll results.

Congress and the president may formulate laws, executive orders, and treaties, but policy is often heavily influenced by ambassadors and the bureaucrats who both inform decision makers and carry out policy. Bureaucrats and diplomats can present skewed information to a decision maker or can carry out a policy in a different way than was intended.

In addition, special-interest groups that provide political support for the party or the officers in power may influence the decision and implementation of policy. For example, an influential leader of an African-American lobby, Randall Robinson, held a personal hunger strike and, many believe, thus influenced President Bill Clinton's decision to intervene in Haiti in 1994.

Economic policy is becoming an increasingly important facet of foreign policy. Certainly there have been times in the past—and will be times in the future—when business representatives will lobby U.S. politicians to carry out or change a certain policy. But many find it surprising that there is a real division of power between the U.S. private and public sectors. In many cases, the interests of a corporation and the government are at odds. However, it is probably safe to say that, whereas

---

12. Jost, "Foreign Policy and Public Opinion," 603, 608.

specific companies may not wield unchecked influence with the government, the *overall* economic well-being of the nation is extremely influential in the formulation of U.S. foreign policy. Many policies are created to help U.S. business, in general, get ahead in the global economy. Thus, U.S. foreign economic policy is inextricably tied to U.S. domestic economic policy.

In short, a number of domestic actors, events, and circumstances heavily influence U.S. foreign policy. Some have suggested that democracies—by encouraging openness and opposition—are influenced in more decisions by more domestic forces or "subnational actors" than are authoritarian regimes.[13] In the case of the United States, this suggestion is true.

Related information: questions 26, 50, 65

60 :
Why does America impose economic sanctions on countries in response to noneconomic situations, such as "undemocratic practices" and "human-rights violations?" Do they really work?

Economic sanctions have long been used by various governments to coerce cooperation.[14] Compared to other nations, the United States has used economic sanctions frequently in response to terrorism, nuclear-arms development, undemocratic practices, human-rights violations, and other activities it deems undesirable. The U.S. government generally uses economic sanctions in such cases to put economic pressure on the consumers and merchants of a target country, who will then put political pressure on the country's leaders to comply with U.S. government stipulations relating to a particular issue.

---

13. Rourke, *International Politics*, 85–112; see especially page 90.

14. The following served as a general source for the information contained in this response: Mary H. Cooper, "Economic Sanctions: Can They Replace Combat in the Post-Cold War Era?" *CQ Researcher* 4, no. 40 (28 October 1994): 937–60.

Sanctions have fulfilled their purposes in some cases. In combination with other factors, sanctions posed against Poland and South Africa accelerated the weakening of those countries' economies and, thereby, helped nudge the ruling parties toward reform and democratic elections, in 1989 and 1994, respectively.

However, critics of sanctions, including many Americans, argue that success stories are relatively few. They say sanctions are often not adequately enforced and, therefore, are ineffectual. For example, some claim the embargo against Cuba (in place since 1962) has failed to force democratic reform because nations that originally agreed to the embargo are now trading with and investing in Cuba. Sanctions can take a great deal of time to have the desired effect on a society and its decision makers; some countries simply become impatient and recommence trade with the targeted country. Many believe Serbian leaders were able to remain defiant years after the United Nations Security Council imposed strict economic sanctions on Serbia and Montenegro (1992) because of political will as well as "porous borders"—informal contraband routes and other sanctions-busting activities by non-Serbs in nearby countries.

Many believe the outcomes do not compensate for the damage that sanctions impose on a society. Critics say the poor suffer under sanctions while political leaders remain unaffected in their ability to meet their basic needs; therefore, sanctions are as undemocratic as the regimes they are meant to punish. Before former President Jimmy Carter negotiated an agreement with the Haitian junta in 1994, he criticized U.S. sanctions against Haiti, claiming they hurt the poorest citizens. The embargo eliminated approximately 60,000 assembly jobs in Haiti's capital, and the average annual income in Haiti decreased by almost half.[15] Embargoes can also hurt U.S. businesses and cost U.S. workers jobs. And critics say sanctions punish the target country's entrepreneurial middle class—the very people who could someday form the country's democratic base.

---

15. Michael Elliott, "Can Haiti Be Saved?" *Newsweek* 124, no. 14 (3 October 1994): 35; Eleanor Clift, "A Man with a Mission," *Newsweek* 124, no. 14 (3 October 1994): 37.

Even in the face of criticism, American policy makers continue to impose economic sanctions, and many believe the use of sanctions will grow among the international community. Compared to military or other types of intervention, sanctions cost governments fairly little (in terms of human and other resources) to impose. They also have the potential to become increasingly effective in a world that is increasingly interdependent economically. However, the United States will have to gain the cooperation of other nations if it wants sanctions to have a significant impact; with competition growing in the global economy, nations may be more willing to gain an advantage by trading with nations punished by sanctions. But multinational cooperation seems much more likely these days: now that Russia and the United States are no longer ideological enemies, proposed sanctions will likely pass the vote of the United Nations Security Council much more readily.

Related information: questions 53, 61

61 : *How do you explain America's inconsistent policy on sanctions against countries with human-rights abuses, authoritarian juntas, etc.?*

America's inconsistent policies relating to human-rights violations and authoritarian regimes is difficult to understand—even for many Americans. As one scholar has noted, political biases and domestic political concerns often cause countries to be "selectively shocked" by human-rights abuses or other undemocratic activities.[16] For example, the United States has simultaneously maintained sanctions against Cuba and cordial trade and diplomatic relations with other regimes that many believe are just as authoritarian. The United States continues to grant China most-favored-nation (MFN) trade status even though the Chinese government denies many of its citizens certain basic human rights. During

---

16. Rourke, *International Politics*, 564.

the Cold War, the U.S. government helped support the Augusto Pinochet regime in Chile and other oppressive regimes in Latin America, largely because the United States perceived them to be anticommunist. And the United States maintains friendly relations with Saudi Arabia, which is a dictatorial monarchy, and Egypt and India, whose governments have failed to punish what many believe to be grievous human-rights abuses against women.

Obviously, the United States maintains relations with governments that have dismal human-rights records in an attempt to protect its economic and political interests. Therefore, many have accused the United States of hypocrisy, which they claim undermines the United States's moral leadership in the world. This point has merit; a completely consistent and evenhanded set of requirements for maintaining diplomatic and economic relations would support the moral viability of U.S. stances and policies.

However, it bears pointing out that, in this increasingly interdependent world, political choices appear to be more complex than ever. More and more interests must be taken into account when formulating trade and other policies. These multiple and often conflicting issues affect priorities and create inconsistencies.

The example of U.S.-China economic relations is an interesting one. The United States grants MFN trade status to all but a few nations; the granting or withholding of that status can have serious implications for a country's economic development. When Bill Clinton ran for president, he was critical of President George Bush's failure to take a stance on human-rights violations in China and claimed he would link China's trade status to its human-rights record. Clinton and his supporters believed doing so would send a message to China that it was accountable for its record; they also believed the United States would be a more credible champion of human rights by taking a firm stand.

However, when China did not bow to pressure and make significant improvements in the field of human rights, Clinton faced a difficult decision. He could have followed through with his threat to sanction

China, but that would have had several serious consequences. U.S. businesses would have faced losses and employees would have lost jobs, not only because of U.S. sanctions but because of possible retaliation by the Chinese government through higher tariffs on U.S. goods. In addition, Clinton had reason to doubt the cooperation of other nations in sanctioning China and, in the absence of that cooperation, U.S. sanctions might have proven ineffectual.

Opponents of sanctions also argued that trade with the West pushes China toward a more democratic system. Many believe Western investment in and interaction with China teaches democratic principles to Chinese workers. They hope China's introduction to capitalism will lead to the development of a working middle class that will demand greater democracy and protection of individual rights.[17] And many believe, if U.S. and Chinese leaders cooperate in the economic arena, political cooperation might be more likely. Indeed, a denial of MFN status might simply antagonize those vying for leadership after Deng Xiaoping's death and create a political atmosphere even more hostile to democracy.[18]

Clinton eventually announced, to the dismay of American human-rights advocates, that he would delink the issues of trade and human rights in China and grant the country MFN status, leaving the door open for further talks on human rights. This is just one example of the numerous factors that can affect the United States's decision to impose sanctions. The fact that numerous, often conflicting interests and issues surround decisions these days makes it much more difficult for nations to have cut-and-dried policies of any kind. And in the absence of cut-and-dried policies, inconsistencies will abound.

Related information: questions 60, 62, 63, 64;

chapter 3 introduction

---

17. Mary H. Cooper, "U.S.-China Trade: Can U.S. Trade Policy Improve Human Rights in China?" *CQ Researcher* 4, no. 14 (15 April 1994): 316–17.

18. Ibid., 321.

62 : *Why does the United States measure other countries by its yardstick with regards to human rights and democracy? Don't you realize strong measures are needed to provide security in some nations?*

The United States does not necessarily measure other countries by its yardstick with regards to human rights and democracy. In the area of human rights, it largely bases its "measurements" on international agreements and standards that many members of the international community endorse. Some of these basic standards are articulated in the Universal Declaration of Human Rights (1948), which is agreed upon— implicitly or explicitly—by all members of the United Nations (UN). Many of the concepts included in the declaration and in subsequent, related documents are regarded as "natural rights"—what some consider to be the Western ideal of the rights individuals had in nature, before communities were organized.[19] However, several non-Western nations have also ratified or acceded to these documents.

Even though many governments have accepted international standards in the areas of human rights and even democracy, they will endorse differing interpretations and practices in relation to these standards. A nation's interpretation often depends on what it most values: individual human rights or collective social order, for example. American culture, law, and institutions have long focused attention on the individual—on his or her rights in relation to the larger community. Many societies, however, share a more group-oriented culture and believe the United States focuses too much on individual rights and not enough on the individual's responsibilities to the community. They argue that the good of a people oftentimes requires greater sacrifice on the part of the individual. For example, an American teenager was caned in Singapore in 1994 for allegedly vandalizing cars. Many Americans, including the president, expressed concern that the caning constituted cruel and unusual punishment and violated the teenager's human rights. How-

19. Rourke, *International Politics*, 213.

ever, Singapore citizens and officials feel maintaining social order some-times requires those who violate that order to pay a painful price. The incident did not cause an irreparable rift in U.S.-Singapore relations, but it did illustrate that countries will often interpret principles differently and that these different interpretations can cause disagreements and tensions.

Certainly, in rare cases, "strong" measures are required to protect national security and even to promote the long-term cause of democ-racy and human rights. The United States has fought wars for such causes, including the U.S. Civil War and World War II. Nevertheless, vigilance with regard to human rights is important under such circumstances. Much of the inspiration for the UN Declaration of Human Rights came from the atrocities committed to humans during World War II. The German government's view of what was justifiable to provide national security had a devastating impact on its targeted populations, the Euro-pean continent, and, indeed, the world. Although Hitler's Germany is an extreme example, it shows how one country's view of justifiable means may be entirely different than that of the majority of the world's nations.

A fine line exists between a government taking strong, *necessary* measures for the long-term good of human rights and democracy and taking strong, *excessive* measures. The International Covenant on Civil and Political Rights, which was drafted after the Universal Declaration, allows that nations may have to take measures during a "public emer-gency which threatens the life of the nation" that would otherwise be condemned by international agreement. Freedom of information and the right of association are just two rights that a government might be justified in suspending when public order is threatened.[20] Temporarily suspending these rights could help protect a people. However, if suspen-sion of rights takes a subtle turn from necessary to excessive, a govern-ment could easily oppress rather than protect. The U.S. government, for example, placed U.S. citizens of Japanese ancestry in detention camps during World War II, thereby denying these people, among other rights,

---

20. Tom J. Farer, "Introduction," in *The International Bill of Human Rights* (Glen Ellen, Calif.: Entwhistle Books, 1981), xix.

the freedom of movement, residence, and association. Ironically, many of these people's sons, brothers, and husbands were fighting for human rights abroad while their families' rights were violated at home. Today, the U.S. government has recognized that these were excessive measures and that it needlessly impinged on the rights of these citizens.

No country, including the United States, measures up to all of the standards outlined in international agreements. Expecting universal compliance may be an unrealistic goal, but if standards do not ensure compliance, at least they establish a mark by which governments are judged and can judge. In agreeing to international standards, all nations give up some sovereignty and state power.[21] Participating countries agree to be watched and to be watchdogs; they are subject to outside pressure to comply that they would not be subject to otherwise, and they are obliged to apply similar pressure to countries not in compliance. Even those countries that have not acceded to such international agreements will be affected by advancing technology and growing multinational trade, organizations, and actions—factors that will increasingly expose "sovereign" governments' actions and policies to international scrutiny.

The United States is not immune from such scrutiny and will be increasingly criticized as well. Again, the United States is far from perfect in upholding and implementing human rights within its own borders or in exacting compliance equally from all nations. The American people and several U.S.-based nongovernmental organizations remain vigilant, watching their own government's actions as well as others'. U.S. governmental and nongovernmental activism often draws criticism that the United States practices "moral imperialism." Nevertheless, many Americans believe some basic human rights are not relative to situation—that some absolute and universal principles help maintain the dignity of the human race—and we all should strive to uphold them, at home as well as abroad.

Related information: question 63

---

21. Peter Meyer, "The International Bill: A Brief History," in *International Bill*, xxiv–xxv.

63 :
Many say America's position on human rights is hypocritical since you still discriminate against minorities in your country. Why does your country police some nations when it is not completely democratic? How does the United States justify passing judgment on other countries?

Some consider the United States to be hypocritical, claiming that Americans fail to practice what they preach. They say Americans hold some nations to a certain standard while holding themselves—and even some of their allies—to another.

The United States has the oldest written constitution that commits to democratic principles, but interpreting and actually implementing its ideals are a constant struggle. No country, including the United States, has been able to achieve "universal coverage" of human rights. The United States may have a procedural democracy, including free elections and a representative government, but it falls short of a substantive democracy, in which all citizens have equal opportunities for education, employment, and other "rights."[22] For America, becoming a democracy has proven to be an evolutionary process. It has taken two hundred years for some principles of the U.S. Constitution to be applied to all U.S. citizens—regardless of race, sex, or religion—and others have yet to achieve universal application.

Until the day comes when the United States is a perfect democracy (and it is doubtful that day will ever come) the United States will continue to function with "blind spots" when it comes to human rights. Indeed, every society has blind spots when considering the ways it oppresses. All people can easily identify the flaws in another society while being unable to see any in their own, largely because of long-standing cultural practices or principles—because the way things are is the way things have always been.

---

22. Rourke, "*International Politics*," 209.

For example, violence against women—particularly by their spouses or partners—is an "accepted custom" in some African, Asian, Latin American and other countries. In some countries, such violence and neglect is even upheld by discriminatory laws.[23] Certainly, the United States does not have a perfect record in protecting women from violence.[24] However, over the last one hundred years, Americans have become more aware of women's human rights, and U.S. laws have moved in the direction of providing equal protection for women and men. When it comes to women's rights, Americans' cultural blind spot is slowly fading.

However, when it comes to other forms of human rights, Americans continue to "walk blindly." Many in economically developing countries argue that Americans impede the rights of the developing world by exploiting natural resources and perpetuating habits of overconsumption that not only exhaust valuable world resources but also damage the world environment. Indeed, studies have shown that the world could not sustain the typical "American lifestyle" if it were practiced worldwide.[25] Still most Americans do not think of consuming more than one hundred pounds of raw materials per day as infringing on others' human rights.[26] When it comes to consumption and waste, Americans have a human-rights blind spot.

America's judgments of other governments would certainly carry more weight if America were free of all injustices. Some accuse U.S. leaders of criticizing other countries' practices while blindly ignoring human-rights violations within their own borders. Others believe America's inattention to domestic problems is more calculated—that the U.S. government is not blind to its country's shortcomings but rather

---

23. Lori Heise, "The Global War against Women," *Utne Reader* no. 36 (November 1989): 40–45, excerpted from *World•Watch* 2, no. 2 (March/April 1989).

24. It is estimated that, in the United States, a woman is beaten every fifteen seconds; statistic cited in Heise, "Global War."

25. Alan Durning, "How Much Is 'Enough?'" *World•Watch* 3, no. 6 (November/December 1990): 14.

26. Ibid., 17.

focuses on other nations' shortcomings to draw attention away from its own human-rights abuses, including inadequate health-care coverage, homelessness, poverty among minority communities, and more.[27]

While these assertions may have some foundation, the accusation that the United States is blind to its own problems—for calculated or more innocent reasons—is not entirely true. In all fairness, it should be noted that Americans admit their inadequacies in achieving universal civil rights, perhaps more freely than citizens of other nations. Most Americans are very aware their nation falls short of the ideal and openly debate America's shortcomings in an attempt to make progress in overcoming them. Many also feel that just because the nation falls short of perfect democracy does not mean America should not maintain some ideals and uphold human rights within and outside of its borders.

Furthermore, America does not demand of other countries civil-rights standards that it does not uphold at home. Most U.S. judgments—in the form of sanctions, for example—are imposed on governments practicing what the U.S. government considers to be extreme human-rights abuses, such as torture, government suppression of political dissidents, undemocratic elections, or imposed authoritarian rule.

Related information: questions 32, 51, 62

64 :   *Why do you continue to pressure and isolate Cuba, even though the Soviet threat no longer exists? You even reconciled with China.*

The U.S. government continues to limit Cuban immigration and uphold a long-standing embargo against Cuba in an attempt to either modify Castro's communist policies or get rid of him altogether.

---

27. Joseph Wronka, *Human Rights and Social Policy in the 21st Century* (Lanham, Md.: University Press of America, Inc., 1992), 232.

In fact, rather than ease restrictions, the government tightened many of them after the Cold War. In 1995, President Bill Clinton reversed a twenty-eight-year-old law that granted political-asylum status to almost all Cuban immigrants. Moreover, a 1992 law prohibits all foreign subsidiaries of U.S. companies from trading with Cuba. These economic and migration restrictions have been tightened to increase the number of political dissidents and keep them in Cuba. U.S. government officials hope that a weakening Cuban economy will create a pressurized political atmosphere to the point that the Cuban people will revolt or otherwise work toward political reform. They believe lifting restrictions or extending aid will only help sustain Castro. They argue that sanctions against Cuba will be dropped only if Castro or a new leader makes substantial democratic and open-market reforms. The U.S. government seems determined: it maintains the embargo even though the United Nations General Assembly continues to condemn it.

Of course, U.S. policy toward Cuba goes beyond a fight against communism and for democratic ideals. To an extent, it stems from a conflict of personality. Castro has been regarded as obstinate and stubborn during his thirty-plus years of dealing with the United States. U.S. officials began talks to normalize relations in the 1970s, but Cuba's public support of Puerto Rican independence and its intervention in the Angolan Civil War antagonized the U.S. government and halted talks. In 1980, the Mariel boat lifts—which brought 120,000 Cubans to Florida—similarly displeased the government. These and other incidents have cast Castro in the role of a spoiler for the U.S. government.

Another factor in maintaining the embargo is the political influence of Cuban exiles. Many of the one-million-plus Cuban Americans live in Florida, a key state in national elections. Though they are torn between wanting relatives to be well-off and wanting Castro out, Cuban Americans are generally pro-embargo and lobby for politicians to keep the pressure on. And that pressure is effective. For example, in the fall of 1995, Clinton was criticized by the leading Republican presidential candidates (who were wooing the Florida vote) after announcing relaxed

U.S. restrictions on travel to Cuba. Other events, such as the Mariel boat lift and the 1994 mass migration of more than 20,000 Cubans, have not won Castro friends among Florida politicians, who had to decide how to fund social services for the immigrants.

Putting diplomatic relations with Cuba on hold is also an act of political and economic expediency. The United States reconciled with China because it needed strategic leverage vis-à-vis the former Soviet Union and access to the huge Chinese market. Simply put, China is a much more powerful political and economic force than Cuba.

Still, some links have been retained between the United States and Cuba, and some are even growing. Since Castro began allowing the importation of dollars from exiled Cubans, the two economies have been linked to a greater extent. Some estimate that exiled Cubans and Cubans who visit the United States contribute nearly one-half billion dollars annually to the Cuban economy—through money and goods shipped to relatives or brought back after visits to the mainland.[28] U.S. telecommunications companies have also developed direct telephone links between the United States and Cuba.

Many Americans, including prominent politicians, would like to see the government lift the embargo. They argue that if the United States extended links to Cuba—through official aid, for example—Castro would be rejected by the people as unnecessary and democratic proponents and ideals would be able to infiltrate the island. They argue that the current embargo only makes the poor poorer, hungrier, and more miserable. Finally, many business representatives claim the embargo costs U.S. businesses billions of dollars, while Europeans and others are free to invest in Cuban enterprises. It will be interesting to see if any of these arguments eventually weakens the will of the U.S. government to reform or depose Castro; similar arguments certainly influenced the Clinton administration to reestablish diplomatic relations with Vietnam (1995).

Related information: question 61

28. Figure estimate by Antonio Jorge, economist at Florida International University, cited in Joel Millman, "Fidel's New Friends," *Forbes* 153, no. 5 (28 February 1994): 66.

65 :
*Will the Middle East peace process that America helped
initiate work? What would the United States do to ensure
peace comes to the Palestinians and Israelis? Haven't you
consistently favored Israel and not adequately considered the
Palestinians?*

Since the end of the Cold War, the world's attention has increasingly
focused on the Middle East. The United States has long had an active
interest in the outcomes of Israeli-Palestinian political struggles and in
the ongoing peace process. It helped bring together Menachem Begin
and Anwar Sadat to sign the Camp David Accords (1978), which provided for Palestinian-Israeli negotiations regarding Israel's occupation of
the West Bank. And U.S. leaders continued to promote discussion between the two groups throughout the next fifteen years. Norway was the
site of final negotiations for a 1993 accord, which prepared the way for
Palestinian self-rule, but the United States was a driving force in promoting and sustaining the talks—a fact that was reinforced by the Yasir
Arafat–Yitzhak Rabin handshake in Washington, D.C.

It would be safe to say that U.S. policy makers have shown a definite pro-Israel bias in the past, and to some extent, that bias still continues. American Jewish organizations and other special-interest groups
supportive of Israel have had a strong influence on U.S. foreign policy
toward Israel. However, many saw the Camp David Accords as a major
step in the United States's recognition of the Palestinian cause and their
rights as a people. Many also believe America's defense of Israel is no
longer unconditional. Oil is a factor; the United States has shown an
expanded awareness of Arab interests—to the point of involving itself in
the Persian Gulf War—because of its dependence on the Middle East's
oil reserves. The *intifada* movement also brought the Palestinian plight
to the attention of the American public and U.S. leaders, who are now
more informed about the legitimacy of Arabic interests. President George
Bush, for example, threatened to cut off hundreds of millions of dollars
in housing loans to Israel if it did not stop building West Bank housing

for Jewish settlers (1990). Congress criticized the threat, and Bush later claimed U.S. policy toward Israel had not changed, but again, many believed the threat signaled a new conditionality regarding U.S. support for Israel.

Arafat's support for Iraq in the Persian Gulf War won him few friends in the United States and may even have lost him a few. However, when he showed himself ready to step back up to the negotiating table, the United States helped facilitate a new round of talks.

Americans will undoubtedly continue to support peace in that region, and the U.S. government will continue to act as a facilitator for negotiations and talks. The United States has also contributed billions of dollars of aid to the region to facilitate development. Much of that aid has gone to Israel, but the Palestinians have also received U.S. funds for economic development, including infrastructure projects in Gaza funded by the U.S.-backed World Bank.

Certainly peace in the region is tenuous, at best. The greatest potential spoilers are Jewish and Islamic extremists who fight the concept of peaceful coexistence. The United States can do little more than offer diplomatic and economic aid. When it comes down to it, the Israelis and Palestinians are the only ones who can ensure that peace comes to the region.[29]

Related information: question 59

66 : *Why are Americans so anti-immigrant? Why do your immigration policies discriminate against immigrants from certain countries?*

Ironically, the United States—a nation made up almost entirely of immigrants—has a history of discriminating against certain immigrant

---

29. Brent Scowcroft, "The Kick-Start that Gave Peace a Chance," *Newsweek* 122, no. 11 (13 September 1993): 27.

groups. The predominant feeling during the United States's first 150 years was that some ethnic groups were genetically and culturally superior to others and that they made better "Americans."[30] Specific laws passed in the late nineteenth and early twentieth centuries created a quota system, which prevented or limited the immigration of peoples from Asia, southern and eastern Europe, and other regions.

However, the U.S. civil rights movement of the 1950s and 1960s, which promoted equal opportunity and protection for minorities, helped spur immigration reform. Laws passed in 1965, 1980, 1986, and 1990 did away with the Western bias of the national-origin quota system. Requirements to obtain an immigrant visa now include (1) having a job skill that fills a need in the United States, (2) reuniting with family members that are legal aliens or citizens, and (3) seeking refuge from political persecution or war.

In the latter half of the twentieth century, these new laws, as well as economic woes and political strife in Asia and Latin America, diversified and increased the flow of immigrants. Between 1981 and 1990, 90 percent of immigrants entering the United States were non-European.[31] Today the United States allows more immigrants to cross its borders than do the other industrialized nations combined.[32] Perhaps U.S. policy seems discriminatory based on individual cases or on publicized stories about persons of color being turned away after entering illegally, but overall, today's immigration laws are fair and nondiscriminatory.

Like the peoples of other countries, Americans' anti-immigrant feelings tend to increase when the economy is stressed and citizens feel there is "not enough to go around." But in general, Americans are more anti-

30. Arthur Mann, "From Immigration to Acculturation," in *Making America: The Society and Culture of the United States*, ed. Luther S. Luedtke (Chapel Hill: University of North Carolina Press, 1992), 71–76.

31. U.S. Immigration and Naturalization Service statistic, cited in *Time Almanac*, 1994 CD-ROM reference ed., s.v. "Immigrants, by Country of Birth: 1961–1991."

32. Tom Morganthau, "America: Still a Melting Pot?" *Newsweek* 122, no. 6 (9 August 1993): 22.

illegal immigration than anti-immigration. Americans in border states particularly feel like they are being overrun. As many as 500,000 illegal immigrants enter the United States annually.[33]

Some Americans believe immigrants are a positive influence—that they contribute culturally and economically to the United States. Others think they drain the U.S. economy. Certainly, with today's government-subsidized welfare programs and higher education costs, immigrants do cost the government more than they did at the beginning of the twentieth century. Some Americans oppose immigration, citing environmental concerns that the country does not have inexhaustible resources and cannot support a rapidly growing population. Others fear immigrants are not assimilating but are guardedly retaining their national characteristics and customs and, thus, compounding ethnic tensions in the United States.

To a certain extent, immigrants become scapegoats for economic and social woes. Even though studies show that, in the long run, immigrants likely pay more in taxes and contribute more to the economy than they take from public funds,[34] people begin to blame immigrants when jobs are scarce, the economy slows, schools run out of money, and crime increases.

The passage of a 1994 California law reflects the fear of immigrants that Americans develop during tough economic times. California has been a "hot spot" because it attracts a large number of immigrants, mostly Asian and Hispanic. With the state's economy weakening, voters placed an initiative on the ballot that would prohibit illegal aliens from receiving government services such as subsidized health care and public education. Opponents of the initiative feared that children would suffer and that the proposition would lead to discrimination against those who looked and/or sound foreign. Although the initiative passed, the law

---

33. Ibid., 20.

34. Mary H. Cooper, "Immigration Reform: Do Immigration Policies Need a Radical Overhaul?" *CQ Researcher* 3, no. 36 (24 September 1993): 846–47.

will likely not go into effect until it is tried before the Supreme Court and ruled constitutional.

Overall, laws are changing to protect legal immigrants against discrimination. A 1986 law attempted to limit illegal immigration, mainly by threatening sanctions against employers who hired illegal aliens (and thus decreasing employment opportunities for illegal aliens). However, when a study showed the law resulted in hiring discrimination against legal immigrants, government officials looked for ways to reform the law. A 1990 immigration law automatically set up a commission to study the law's effects on the immigrant community and the general population. So in general, more safeguards are now in place to ensure that immigration laws do not promote discrimination.

67 . *Why do you send ambassadors who try to intervene in our country and yet know so little about our people, culture, and language?*

U.S. ambassadors are appointed by each president to be his personal representative and to direct the nation's embassy in a foreign capital. The chief responsibility of a U.S. ambassador is to promote and advocate America's national interest—a job that critics sometimes label "intervention." However, the line between advocacy and intervention is fine and is often in the eye of the beholder.

U.S. ambassadors have been accused much less frequently of meddling over the last several decades. It is more difficult for an ambassador to be a power broker now, even if he or she so desires. With increased media coverage of their actions, ambassadors are much more accountable than they once were. Worldwide instantaneous communications also allow senior officials in Washington, D.C., to easily gather information, give detailed instructions, and even manage crises from home, thereby reducing an ambassador's power. And Washington officials can travel abroad more easily and frequently today. Still, ambassadors are valuable as on-site sources of information and negotiators.

While ambassadors have come from a variety of backgrounds, many are career diplomats who resign their foreign-service commissions to accept an ambassador position. Presidents also appoint people who were active in their political campaigns, contributed financially to their political party, or were otherwise influential in helping them "get to the top."

The "disaster" ambassadors of the past have become fewer in number. The U.S. Senate must confirm ambassador appointments and is increasingly demanding. Ambassador nominees must also face media scrutiny, and the host country must find the ambassador acceptable. In short, standards are much higher than they were in the past. Many ambassadors today have a career-long history of diplomatic service in the country or region in which they serve; many are familiar with the host country's language; and most have a reputation as skilled negotiators. It has become more difficult for controversial or incompetent persons to get an ambassadorship.

Once confirmed, the great majority of ambassadors work hard to become acquainted with a country's culture, politics, and leaders—if they are not acquainted already—in order to represent their country reputably. They are assisted by "country teams," which may number several hundred and consist of staff members and career foreign-service officers representing federal organizations active in foreign affairs.

Certainly, some ambassadors have been sent to countries where they are not familiar with the language or culture. The ambassador President Jimmy Carter appointed to Saudi Arabia did not speak Arabic. He had been a state governor and a close associate of Carter during his 1976 presidential campaign. Ambassador John West was effective mainly because the Saudis valued a representative who enjoyed a personal, confidential relationship with the president. He even arranged for Carter to visit Saudi Arabia on one of Carter's first trips abroad as president.

President Bill Clinton named Walter Mondale, past vice president (1976–80) and presidential candidate (1984), as ambassador to Japan

(1993). Mondale had traveled to Japan but was not necessarily an Asianist or fluent in Japanese. Perhaps more importantly, he was a respected politician and was known to talk relatively frequently with Clinton. The appointment of such a high-profile politician was meant to communicate to Japan its importance to U.S. foreign relations. Mondale, known as a skilled negotiator, was appointed when the United States sorely needed to better its economic relations with Japan. So cultural awareness is not the only qualification in being an effective ambassador. Political skills and clout are also crucial.

68 : *Aren't most of the Americans we see in our country— businesspeople, missionaries, Peace Corps volunteers, etc.—involved in intelligence gathering for the CIA?*

In short, no. The vast majority of Americans abroad are not involved in intelligence-gathering activities.

American businesspeople mainly seek overseas opportunities to make a profit. Some may be engaged in development work under government contract and, in that capacity, gather information to help the U.S. government understand a country and its economy better, but they are usually not involved in covert intelligence. For the most part, there is a distinct division between private and public sectors in the United States. The work most private businesspeople do is completely unrelated to government operations.

American missionaries are certainly prevalent worldwide. More missionaries come from the United States than from any other country, and the number of missionaries from U.S. evangelical denominations and U.S.-based proselytizing churches, such as the Church of Jesus Christ of Latter-day Saints (Mormons), is growing.

Most missionaries travel abroad to teach others about their religious beliefs, although many are also involved in humanitarian service, offering education, health-care, and other services. They clearly see themselves as serving a God-appointed, not a government-appointed, mission. In fact, a number of churches explicitly direct missionaries to not involve themselves in the politics of their host countries. At one time, U.S. missionaries were regarded as U.S. agents because they promoted U.S. political and economic philosophies and represented U.S. culture as "God's culture." For the most part, however, these practices have changed. Today, churches and their representatives are much more sensitive to a host country's culture.

The Peace Corps, though government-funded, is an independent organization; it is not controlled by the U.S. Department of State, and its volunteers are not necessarily government careerists. The corps sends out thousands of volunteers each year (about 6,500 are serving at a given time), but they are only placed in a country at the request of that country's government. (Volunteers currently serve in more than ninety countries.) The majority of volunteers are college graduates who enter the corps for a variety of reasons, but spying is not among them. They go for more personal, often more mundane, reasons. Some are not able to find a job after graduation. Others are retired and looking for something worthwhile to do. Some want to gain international experience before beginning graduate school. Others are simply looking for a challenge or an adventure, or they have a conviction that they should serve and make a contribution to the world. The chief goals of the corps are to promote peace throughout the world, help the world's poor meet their basic needs, and increase interaction and understanding between Americans and other peoples—none of which involves covert intelligence activities.

69 : *Why does your country participate in the training of military dictators?*

Each year, thousands of international military personnel come to the United States for training or join with American forces overseas in joint training exercises. These exchange arrangements are often part of larger treaty negotiations or military-sales agreements. Some individuals involved in these exchanges have contributed to dictatorial regimes on returning home, but the vast majority have returned to help modernize their countries' national security systems and further the cause of international cooperation.

Presumably, this question specifically concerns the U.S. Army's elite School of the Americas, which has been in operation since 1946.[35] The school spends about $4 million annually in training Latin American soldiers and has trained tens of thousands of soldiers over the years. Its goals include strengthening democracy in Latin America, increasing professionalism in Latin American armies, and maintaining a measure of U.S. influence in the region.

Over the decades, the school has been harshly criticized as a "school of dictators and thugs." Some of its more infamous alumni include past Panamanian president and drug-ring leader Manuel Noriega; a Guatemalan colonel linked to the deaths of a U.S. innkeeper and a guerrilla insurgent married to an American lawyer; a notorious death-squad leader in El Salvador; nineteen Salvadoranian officers who were involved in killing six Jesuit priests; and a number of other military men accused of corruption and murder in their home countries.

---

35. The following served as general sources for the information contained in this response: James Hodge, "House Efforts to End 'School for Dictators' Funding Fails," *National Catholic Reporter* 29, no. 44 (15 October 1993): 10; Eric Schmitt, "School for Assassins, or Aid to Latin Democracy?" *New York Times*, 3 April 1995, late edition, sec. A; Douglas Waller, "Running a 'School for Dictators,'" *Newsweek* 122, no. 6 (9 August 1993): 34–37.

Critics concede that the school does not teach its students to be corrupt; students usually come with behavioral patterns and moral standards already ingrained in them. However, critics say some students have participated in questionable practices before they arrive, and unfortunately, their participation in the school increases their prestige at home. Critics argue, therefore, that prospective students should be more carefully screened. Others argue that the school is irrelevant in the post-Cold War world. During the Cold War, buying the cooperation of Western-hemisphere neighbors, no matter how unsavory they were, may have been a necessity. But now the United States can and must be more particular about where it invests its money.

Defenders of the school say that, of the more than sixty thousand graduates, only a few hundred have been accused of serious human-rights violations and fewer than one hundred have been convicted. They argue that the school teaches valuable skills to Latin American leaders and, increasingly, teaches them valuable ethics as well. In fact, the school now includes an expanded human-rights curriculum. Supporters also say the United States's need to retain a presence in Latin America did not end with the Cold War. Closing the school would eliminate one way the United States can extend its influence in a growing and developing region.

In 1993, a group of congressional representatives attempted to cut off funding for the school, claiming the institution links the United States with "tyranny and oppression." The attempt failed, but the vote was closer than many expected. As military spending is cut and the American people call for the government to invest more money at home, the school may indeed lose its funding one day. Relatively little of the U.S. military budget is spent on the school, but it has become increasingly criticized over the last several decades, and its reputation marks it as a high-profile target for budget cuts.

70 :
Given the fact that the majority of world resources are consumed by developed countries and these countries are responsible for major global environmental degradation, what is the U.S. government doing to preserve the global environment? What is it doing to clean up the environmental mess in areas such as eastern Europe and Latin America?

Many believe Americans are not acting with urgency in the environmental arena. The fact that the United States is geographically isolated—compared to European countries, for example—does tend to downplay the urgency and necessity of international environmental action. President George Bush, in particular, was criticized concerning his participation in the 1989 United Nations Conference on Environment and Development, also known as the Rio Conference or Earth Summit. He was regarded as inflexible in meeting the demands of less-developed countries relating to issues such as developing nations' responsibilities for pollution control. Indeed, Bush's posture at the conference was considered by many to be pro-business and anti-environment, and it caused an international scandal.

The U.S. government has shown itself to be pro-environment in other ways. It has donated hundreds of millions of dollars to eastern Europe for environmental cleanup, though the extensive and expensive nature of the problem means the funds do not go far. The United States has filtered some money filtered through the World Bank (in which the United States is a principal investor), which has loaned billions of dollars for cleanup efforts in Latin American and European countries. In fact, many World Bank loans are now linked to recipient countries tightening their environmental standards. The United States Agency for International Development (USAID) also gives grants and loans for conservation efforts, such as tree-planting projects, throughout the world.

In 1991, President Bush introduced the Enterprise of the Americas Initiative, which called for restructuring Latin America's debt, allowing countries to reduce their debt while investing the interest in environ-mental funds. This was done to reduce governments' tendencies to (1) ex-ploit their natural resources to service their debts and (2) spend money in debt payments that should be used to protect resources. For example, in 1991, the U.S. government announced it would cancel Bolivia's nearly $350 million debt from U.S. assistance programs. The agreement stipu-lated that, in return, over the next decade, Bolivia's government was to invest $20 million in environmental projects.

The United States has also joined environmental efforts with other governments. In an attempt to stretch aid money further, representa-tives from North America (including the United States), Europe, and Japan agreed to support the Environmental Action Program in 1993; this program was designed to reverse the effects of pollution in eastern Europe. The governments pledged $30 million in technical assistance that would fund small-scale projects with potentially large returns.

In addition to U.S. government activities, U.S. business and non-governmental organizations (NGOs) have aided environmental activi-ties abroad. Some NGOs are involved in debt-for-nature swaps. They buy a portion of a country's debt from a bank and then formulate a new loan agreement, on the condition that the government carries out an environmental project. Other U.S.-based organizations, such as the World Wildlife Fund, World Resources Institute, Audubon Society, and Sierra Club, also sponsor environmental cleanup and preservation programs abroad.

U.S. businesses, ranging from candy to clothing companies, manu-facture products using renewable resources from such places as the Brazilian rain forest in an effort to motivate natives to preserve those resources. Some companies even donate a portion of their profits to pre-serving the rain forest or other environmental causes. U.S. businesses also offer environmental consulting services abroad, particularly in east-ern Europe, and sell modern, clean technology to countries that have antiquated pollution-control technology. U.S. technology tends to be relatively inexpensive in comparison to that sold by other countries. And some U.S. companies offer cheap but effective cleanup services, such as landfills.

There is also good news regarding Americans' efforts to clean up and preserve the environment at home. In the United States, the air is cleaner, the rain less acidic, and the forests more plentiful than they have been in decades.[36] Still, admittedly, the United States could do much more at home and abroad to help preserve the global environment. Perhaps as the consequences of global pollution begin reaching America's borders, Americans will further abandon their isolationist tendencies and become more involved in global environmental causes.

Related information: questions 18, 51

---

36. Gregg Easterbrook, *A Moment on the Earth: The Coming Age of Environmental Optimism* (New York: Viking, 1995), cited in Robert J. Samuelson, "The Rise of 'Ecorealism': Let's Not Deny Good News about the Environment," *Newsweek* 125, no. 15 (10 April 1995): 46.

EPILOGUE

EPILOGUE

FURTHER GUIDELINES
for PRACTICING
CITIZEN DIPLOMACY

Perhaps the most constructive goal one could set as a citizen diplomat is to "shatter the stereotype." As a people, Americans have a long-standing reputation of being ethnocentric, loud, demanding, and impatient—in short, obnoxious. Whether the "ugly American" label is deserved or undeserved is not the question. The question is, how can we stop the perpetuation of the stereotype and replace it with a more positive perception? Implementing the following guidelines can help. Though most of the guidelines discuss travel abroad, many of the principles can be applied to interaction with international visitors in the United States.

Become Culture Wise

If you are hosting international visitors, learn about the positive and significant aspects of their culture before they arrive. Doing some prior research will help you be a better, more sensitive host. Asking them appropriate, specific questions and showing an interest in their culture after their arrival will also give your guests entree to asking you questions about America and, thus, open an effective means of cultural interchange.

If you are traveling abroad, learn as much as you can about your destination before you leave: the current social conditions, people, history, transportation systems, communications systems, common gestures and sayings, health-care facilities, diet, etc. Prior knowledge about even the most practical things can save you from spending all of your time being "put out" or frustrated. If buses regularly break down or run late, you can schedule accordingly. If the local diet consists mainly of spicy foods, you can pack a supply of antacid. And knowing beforehand which gestures are common and which are considered crude can save you from offending someone and embarrassing yourself.

STUDY A VARIETY OF MATERIALS

Sources of cultural information are widely available, from travel books and briefings, to videos and computer on-line services, to free information provided by many embassies. Whatever you access, choose more than one source to help you avoid forming stereotypes.

The David M. Kennedy Center for International Studies publishes more than 160 four-page *Culturgrams* that contain information about cultures worldwide. These briefings provide valuable insights into your questioners' country and cultural background, including their lifestyles and customs. The *United States Culturgram for the International Visitor* is an expanded, six-page briefing that contains information on U.S. history, government, peoples, customs, and lifestyles. You may want to obtain one for yourself if traveling abroad or for an international visitor you are hosting. As of 1997, this publication was available in English, French, German, Italian, Japanese, Polish, Portuguese, Russian, and Spanish.

Intercultural Interacting, a one-hundred-page book, offers general guidelines for communicating with people from other cultures. It too is published by the Kennedy Center. For more information about the Center's publications, contact: Kennedy Center Publications, Brigham Young University, PO Box 24538, Provo, UT 84602-4538; phone (800) 528-6279; fax (801) 378-5882; web: www.byu.edu/culturgrams.

In addition to learning about other countries, you may feel a need to brush up on your own culture, government, and society. When discussing the United States, most non-Americans are not interested in personal political statements or lengthy reports. They are looking for an easily remembered, concise response they can use in future conversations. However, if you want to be better informed or need exact information, the following sources may be of help.

Official U.S. Department of State publications can help you better understand and answer questions about specific government policies and actions—particularly those that affect other countries. These publications are available in a number of formats.

If you find yourself traveling regularly as an "unofficial representative" of the United States, you may want to subscribe to the *U.S. Department of State Dispatch*, a weekly publication that is the official record of U.S. foreign policy. It contains official statements, speeches, fact sheets, treaty actions, country profiles, and other reports. For ordering information, contact: Superintendent of Documents, U.S. Government Printing Office (GPO), PO Box 371954, Pittsburgh, PA 15250-7954; phone (202) 512-1800. *Dispatch* and other State Department publications are also available in most federal depository libraries and some public and university libraries.

The Department of State Foreign Affairs Network (DOSFAN) on the Internet provides official U.S. foreign policy information. DOSFAN is updated daily and contains country- and issue-specific information; *Dispatch*, *Background Notes* on countries and organizations; international business information; congressional reports on trade, human rights, and more; and other official publications and pronouncements. This Internet service is a cooperative effort between the Office of Public Communication's Bureau of Public Affairs and the University of Illinois at Chicago. DOSFAN, is accessible through one of the following electronic addresses: *Gopher* dosfan.lib.uic.edu; *URL* gopher://dosfan.lib.uic.edu/; *WWW* http://dosfan.lib.uic.edu/dosfan.html. For assistance or information, contact the project coordinator by e-mail at john.a.shuler@uic.edu or call (312) 996-2738.

The Bureau of Public Affairs also offers a fax-on-demand service, which provides, for the cost of a long-distance telephone call, facsimile copies of major speeches, selected reports and fact sheets, etc. For information, call the Public Information Division, Bureau of Public Affairs, at (202) 647-6575. A Federal Bulletin Board Service provides foreign policy information by modem. For information, call the GPO's Office of Electronic Information Dissemination Services at (202) 512-1530. To order U.S. foreign affairs information on CD-ROM, contact the Superintendent of Documents at the address or telephone number on page 205.

You can also obtain domestic and foreign policy information by submitting a request to your congressional representatives.

Your local library may subscribe to other publications that address American societal trends, domestic and foreign policy, treaties, laws, and trade relations. *The CQ Researcher* is a valuable resource found in some libraries. Published four times monthly, *CQ Researcher* offers a concise but thorough examination of current issues and events—domestic and international. These twenty-page briefings are designed as a starting place for research and contain annotated bibliographies of books and articles for further reference.

When searching abroad for information about the United States, you may want to contact the nearest office or library of the U.S. Information Agency or the U.S. embassy. Before leaving the United States, obtain the names and addresses of foreign service officers who provide assistance to U.S. citizens overseas. *Key Officers of Foreign Service Posts— Guide for Business Representatives*, a resource available at some libraries, is published twice a year and lists the names, telephone numbers, and fax numbers of these officers at U.S. embassies, missions, consulates general, and consulates. This information is also available through DOSFAN.

KEEP YOUR EYES AND MIND WIDE OPEN

While you are away from home, notice everything, absorb everything. Continue to learn about the people's worldview and culture, and compare and contrast them with your own. Because differences are often more "glaring," make a concerted effort to identify similarities with various aspects of U.S. culture. And because differences can seem repugnant (by the very fact that they are different), look for different practices and priorities that are admirable or even worthy of emulation. Avoid the temptation of passing judgment on cultural differences with an automatic and sweeping "our way is better." One of the most important phrases to erase from your vocabulary is "But in America we . . . ."

As much as you try to prepare yourself or keep an open mind, you will encounter frustrations, just as you do at home. Do not let minor frustrations with individuals or the "system" annoy you to the point of condemning the culture. Remember that frustrations also occur at home. Flexibility with self, others, and circumstances is key.[1]

Mingle

While you needn't "go native" when visiting another country, you can make an effort to step out of your comfort zone. If they are generally considered safe, take buses instead of taxis. If you are language capable, go where the locals, not Americans, socialize. Shop in local markets. Eat local delicacies (again, if they are considered safe). Watch local television. Try using the local language, even if—*especially* if—your skills are limited. Most people are happy to help you learn the language if you show a genuine interest. They see it as an attempt on your part to learn more about their culture.

As you interact with people in the local culture, be aware of the tone of voice and body language people use. Joking rambunctiously and gesturing wildly while talking with friends on a bus may be acceptable in Jersey City but not in Guatemala City. An excellent rule of thumb is just try to blend in with others.

In addition, as you mingle with locals, be prepared for questions about the United States. People will expect you to know about American culture, society, government—even economics and foreign policy.

---

1. V. Lynn Tyler, *Intercultural Interacting* (Provo, Utah: David M. Kennedy Center for International Studies Publications Services, 1987), 44–45.

Reading this book can help prepare you to respond appropriately to the questions that will inevitably come your way.

RECORD YOUR REACTIONS

You may want to take pictures of things that strike you as similar to and different from home: dining places and practices, homes, home decor, dress, transportation and communication systems, etc. (Ask permission before taking pictures of people, their homes, or their possessions; people on the street may ask you to pay for taking their picture.) Record your reaction to each picture, and then, at a later time, reevaluate those reactions. You will likely find that your views of the culture have changed.

Many travelers also recommend keeping a journal and referring to it occasionally to understand how and why your attitudes change over time.

SHARE INTERNATIONAL EXPERIENCES AND MEMORIES

After traveling or living abroad, you can take home a greater appreciation for your host country and share it with others. Encourage your friends and neighbors to learn more, but not necessarily with an endless slide show. Share what people ask about—a favorite picture, a local dish, a traditional song, one story. You may simply want to visit with family, friends, and associates about your experiences and encourage questions. Just remember that a little knowledge can go a long way; those with greater interest will ask for more. You won't want to convey an air of superiority that could cause resentment. However, if you do not engage in some reflective conversation after your visit, you lose out on a learning experience, as do those with whom you associate and those who may travel to the same area.

Some libraries and universities sponsor intercultural education programs. They recruit people who have lived in other countries to do cultural presentations in public libraries or classrooms. You may want to check with a local library or university to see if such a program exists in your area.

If you have associates who just returned from a trip abroad, ask them about their experience. Because they fear being a "bore," many do not share their experiences unless someone directly asks them to do so.

Maintaining friendships with people you meet abroad is another way to share memories. Staying in touch opens the way for a continuous flow of intercultural communication and education long after you have returned home.

BE A LIFELONG STUDENT

Developing an "expertise" on a given culture, country, or region can be personally satisfying and valuable in practicing citizen diplomacy. However, becoming an expert is a difficult task, requiring continued—even lifelong—interest and study. So travel. Continue to read books about peoples and places that interest you. Search out and speak with people from those places who are traveling, studying, or working in the United States. Again, keep in touch with people you meet in your travels; maintaining these contacts will help you keep abreast of recent trends and happenings in their countries and will broaden your understanding.

Above all, remain teachable. After all, many of the best citizen diplomats are those who consider themselves "students of the world."